James C. Morris

EPISTLE TO THE ROMANS

Copyright © 2022, James C. Morris

Epistle to the Romans

Scripture taken from the New King James Version.
Copyright © 1979, 1980, 1982 by Thomas Nelson, Inc.
Used by permission. All rights reserved.

Bible text from the New King James Version is not to be reproduced in copies or otherwise by any means except as permitted in writing by Thomas Nelson, Inc., Attn: Bible Rights and Permissions, P.O. Box 141000, Nashville, TN 37214-1000.

ISBN: 978-1-945774-79-9

Trust House Publishers

P.O. Box 3181

Taos, NM 87571

www.trusthousepublishers.com

Ordering Information: Special discounts are available on quantity purchases by churches, associations, and retailers. For details, contact the publisher at the address above or call toll-free 1-844-321-4202.

1 2 3 4 5 6 7 8 9

TABLE OF CONTENTS

PREFACE 1

THE INTRODUCTION
Romans 1:1-17 3

Section 1
CHAPTER 1:18 - 8:39
The Romans Road 7

SECTION 2
CHAPTERS 9-11
God's Reliability 39

SECTION 3
CHAPTER 12:1 - 15:13
Christian Service 87

CONCLUSION
Chapters 15:14 - 16:27 101

PREFACE

In examining the Epistle to the Romans, it is important to remember that the division of the Bible into chapters and verses is a human innovation, something not included in the texts as originally given by God. So in considering this important epistle, we need to see the sections into which the Holy Spirit divided it, and treat each of these sections as a whole, and not just treat it on the basis of chapters and verses. And it is in view of dealing with these sections as a whole that this book is written. So no attempt has been made to wring the last drop of truth from any part of this epistle. Instead, the purpose of this book is to demonstrate the overall message of each section of the Epistle to the Romans, and to show how that overall message is developed and presented. So the parts of the epistle necessary to see these overall messages are treated in detail. But other parts are sometimes skipped over. This is not because these other parts are of lessor importance, but because concentrating on details can sometimes make it more difficult to follow the overall message contained in a larger portion of the word of God.

In addition to a short introduction and a rather extended conclusion, this important epistle is divided into three main sections. The first section, chapters 1-8, traces the normal development of a Christian, from his original realization of his guilt before a Holy God, to full maturity in Christ. The second section, chapters 9-11, demonstrates the absolute reliability of God's promises by assuring us that the ancient and rebellious nation of Israel has not been given up. That God will, even yet, eventually keep the promises He made so long ago to that guilty nation. For many of these promises had been made even as He was announcing that nation's destruction because of its wickedness. And the third section, chapters 12-15, covers Christian service. While this might seem to be unrelated to the previous sections, in truth this is only a practical outworking of the truths presented in the first two sections.

THE INTRODUCTION

Romans 1:1-17

In the first verse, Paul states his authority in writing this epistle. **"Paul, a bondservant of Jesus Christ, called** *to be* **an apostle, separated to the gospel of God."** (Romans 1:1) Paul's authority lay in the fact that he was **"a bondservant of Jesus Christ,"** a **"called apostle"** (notice that the words **"***to be***"** are in italics, meaning that they were not in the original Greek text,) and that he had been **"separated to the gospel of God."** Having been **"called"** as **"an apostle"** and **"separated to the gospel"** were what gave Paul his authority. For all true spiritual authority comes directly from God. And being **"a bondservant of Jesus Christ"** meant that he had a duty to say only what he had been told to say.

The seventh verse states to whom this epistle is addressed. **"To all who are in Rome, beloved of God, called** *to be* **saints:"** (Romans 1:7a) In the original Greek, this sentence does not contain the breaks indicated by the commas, nor does it contain the words **"***to be***,"** which, as we have noticed, is why they are in italics. We notice these details to understand that this epistle was not addressed to all the inhabitants of the city of Rome, as well as those **"beloved of God"** and **"called** *to be* **saints."** Rather, it is addressed **"To all who are in Rome"** that are **"beloved of God"** and **"called saints."** For this is not a statement that we are **"called** *to be* **saints,"** but rather that we are **"called"** *as* **"saints."** Or, as we might say, we are saints by calling.

That is, this is not an observation that these beloved people had been commanded to live holy lives, although they had indeed been so commanded. Instead, this is an observation that they had already been made holy by the calling that God had placed upon their lives. And, rather than being addressed to all the citizens of Rome, the particular Romans to whom this epistle was addressed were these **"beloved" "saints."**

Then, as in almost all of his epistles, Paul begins with a commendation of the ones he is exhorting. **"First, I thank my God through Jesus Christ for you all, that your faith is spoken of throughout the whole world."** (Romans 1:8) It has often been noticed that this kind of opening was normal for the epistles of Paul, being present in all his epistles to churches except the one to the Galatians.[1] But here we need to notice a second detail that has largely been missed. For the conclusion of this epistle begins with the words **"Now I myself am confident concerning you, my brethren, that you also are full of goodness, filled with all knowledge, able also to admonish one another."** (Romans 15:14) This sandwiching of the basic message between statements of praise toward those being addressed is not just an effective psychological trick, but an example for ministry in all times. For if people are only made to feel condemned, they feel an internal resistance to whatever they are being told. But if they are made to feel loved and accepted, they are much more receptive to both instruction and correction.

The remainder of the introduction treats of the Apostle's great desire to come to Rome and to personally minister to the spiritual needs of the saints there. And this could indeed have been the desire of the Holy Spirit as well. But this was prevented from taking place by the disobedience of the Apostle himself, as will be treated more completely when we get to the conclusion of this epistle, where Paul's desire in this matter was discussed in greater detail.

---

1   It has often been observed that the reason there is no commendation in the epistle to the Galatians was because of the seriousness of the false doctrine being taught there. In addressing that false doctrine, the Apostle went so far as to say, **"I desire to be present with you now, and to change my voice; for I stand in doubt of you."** (Galatians 4:20) So the error being treated in that epistle was so grave as to amount to a repudiation of basic Christian doctrine. So serious that it made the Apostle doubt that these people were actual believers in the gospel of Jesus Christ.

SECTION

CHAPTER 1:18 – 8:39

The Romans Road

The first eight chapters of the book of Romans take us sequentially through the normal development of a Christian, from his first realization of his guilt before God to full maturity in Christ.

After the introduction, the first chapter of this important epistle gives us God's unsparing condemnation of those who are openly wicked. Then, in the second chapter, we find His far more severe condemnation of those who imagine themselves to be better than those openly wicked people. Finally, in the third chapter the condemnation spreads out to all mankind.

And then justification by faith is presented from the last part of chapter three through chapter four. In chapter five, this produces peace with God, in confident assurance of salvation through His blood.

But then, in chapter six, the new believer is warned of the need to live a holy life. This is not presented as something that would merely be beneficial or desirable, but as a requirement, something that is absolutely necessary. And chapter seven takes up what happens when a person sets out to do this. The struggle is described in detail, basically showing that this is impossible. That, no matter how hard we might try, *we* are unable to live this holy life that is *required* in a Christian, and that every true believer in Christ so greatly desires to live.

If the message stopped there, we would be left completely hopeless. For we realize that *we* are simply unable to live the life that our God requires from us. But the eighth chapter of Romans finally gives us the secret. *We* will never succeed in living the holy life required of us, but *He* can do that very thing through us. *We* need to forget about ourselves, and get our eyes on *Him*. As long as *we* try to be holy, we will never succeed. But when we forget about ourselves, and instead fill our hearts and minds with *Him*, we will live holy lives without even trying to do it.

And *that* is the real, central, message of these eight chapters, which have come to be called "the Romans road."

So in examining this, we need to start with God's unsparing condemnation of the wicked.

> **"For the wrath of God is revealed from heaven against all ungodliness and unrighteousness of men, who suppress the truth in unrighteousness, because what may be known of God is manifest in them, for God has shown *it* to them. For since the creation of the world His invisible *attributes* are clearly seen, being understood by the things that are made, *even* His eternal power and Godhead, so that they are without excuse, because, although they knew God, they did not glorify *Him* as God, nor were thankful, but became futile in their thoughts, and their foolish hearts were darkened. Professing to be wise, they became fools, and changed the glory of the incorruptible God into an image made like corruptible man--and birds and four-footed animals and creeping things."** (Romans 1:18-23)

We need to notice here that the basic, the *root* sin that God is here condemning, is not the open wickedness that we so commonly condemn as unacceptable. Instead, here God goes down to the very *root* of the problem. And that *root* is a decision by mankind that they simply do not *want* God. The condemnation is not that they had committed certain sins, but rather that they knew about God, and had *wilfully* turned away from that knowledge.

And what is God's reaction to such a conscious decision? Other scriptures state it clearly in regard to a time coming on this earth. For Isaiah 66:3b-4 says, **"Just as they have chosen their own ways, And their soul delights in their abominations, So will I choose their delu-**

sions, And bring their fears on them; Because, when I called, no one answered, When I spoke they did not hear; But they did evil before My eyes, And chose *that* in which I do not delight." A similar warning is found in 2 Thessalonians 2:9-12, where we read that "The coming of the *lawless one* is according to the working of Satan, with all power, signs, and lying wonders, and with all unrighteous deception among those who perish, because they did not receive the love of the truth, that they might be saved. And for this reason God will send them strong delusion, that they should believe the lie, that they all may be condemned who did not believe the truth but had pleasure in unrighteousness."

In each of these cases, God very clearly said that He will impose spiritual blindness upon certain people because they have consciously rejected His message. That is, not because they had simply neglected His message, but because they had decided that they did not want His message. And the last part of Romans 1 says the same about mankind in general. So we read, keeping the previous verses of this chapter in mind,

> "Therefore God also gave them up to uncleanness, in the lusts of their hearts, to dishonor their bodies among themselves, who exchanged the truth of God for the lie, and worshiped and served the creature rather than the Creator, who is blessed forever. Amen. For this reason God gave them up to vile passions. For even their women exchanged the natural use for what is against nature. Likewise also the men, leaving the natural use of the woman, burned in their lust for one another, men with men committing what is shameful, and receiving in themselves the penalty of their error which was due. And even as they did not like to retain God in *their* knowledge, God gave them over to a debased mind, to do those things which are not fitting; being filled with all unrighteousness, sexual immorality, wickedness, covetousness, maliciousness; full of envy, murder, strife, deceit, evil-mindedness; *they are* whisperers, backbiters, haters of God, violent, proud, boasters, inventors of evil things, disobedient to parents, undiscerning, untrustworthy, unloving, unforgiving, unmerciful; who, knowing the righteous judgment of God, that those who practice such things are deserving of death, not only do the same but also approve of those who practice them." (Romans 1:24-32)

It would be difficult for any of us to find words that would be more brutal and unsparing in condemning such wickedness as is described here. But in the midst of this condemnation, we need to notice that this lack of even a basic moral understanding in these people does not just happen by chance. Instead, God very clearly said that He *inflicts* this blindness upon people *as a punishment*.

Although the reason for this judgment by God is not stated at this place in the scriptures, it is clearly stated in other places, such as **"Serpents, brood of vipers! How can you escape the condemnation of hell? Therefore, indeed, I send you prophets, wise men, and scribes: *some* of them you will kill and crucify, and *some* of them you will scourge in your synagogues and persecute from city to city, that on you may come all the righteous blood shed on the earth, from the blood of righteous Abel to the blood of Zechariah, son of Berechiah, whom you murdered between the temple and the altar."** (Matthew 23:33-35) So we see that, when God has decided to judge a person (or a group) for the sin of rejecting Himself, He condemns them to expose their guilt in such a way that it becomes evident to all, even to themselves, thus making it obvious that His judgment is just.

The scriptures also give us another warning about wilfully turning away from the truth of God, as follows.

> **"For *it is* impossible for those who were once enlightened, and have tasted the heavenly gift, and have become partakers of the Holy Spirit, and have tasted the good word of God and the powers of the age to come, if they fall away, to renew them again to repentance, since they crucify again for themselves the Son of God, and put *Him* to an open shame. For the earth which drinks in the rain that often comes upon it, and bears herbs useful for those by whom it is cultivated, receives blessing from God; but if it bears thorns and briars, *it is* rejected and near to being cursed, whose end *is* to be burned."** (Hebrews 6:4-8)

So we see that the scriptures indeed teach, and very plainly teach, that it is a very serious thing to choose pleasure over God. And if that choice is made consciously, and with a sense of finality, if we push

God too far, He will eventually say, "Very well. You don't want Me? Fine. Do your own thing. We will deal with that later."

And when that happens, all hope is lost. For the scriptures plainly say, **"For by grace you have been saved through faith, and that not of yourselves;** *it is* **the gift of God,"** (Ephesians 2:8) and **"do you despise the riches of His goodness, forbearance, and longsuffering, not knowing that the goodness of God leads you to repentance?"** (Romans 2:4) In the first of these we see that even the faith to believe the gospel is a gift from God. And in the second we see that it is **"the goodness of God"** that **"leads you to repentance."** So if God turns away from you, there is no more hope. Such a person **"is rejected and near to being cursed, whose end** *is* **to be burned."** And that is why, for such people, **"***it is* **impossible... to renew them again to repentance."**

We have examined various aspects of this last part of Romans 1. But we need now to turn back to its basic message. For we must not lose sight of the fact that, although all these other aspects are both true and important, the basic message of this section is God's unsparing condemnation of the wicked. This is because the subject of the second chapter of Romans is His far more unsparing condemnation of those who imagine themselves to be better than these openly wicked people.

> **"Therefore you are inexcusable, O man, whoever you are who judge, for in whatever you judge another you condemn yourself; for you who judge practice the same things. But we know that the judgment of God is according to truth against those who practice such things. And do you think this, O man, you who judge those practicing such things, and doing the same, that you will escape the judgment of God?"** (Romans 2:1-3)

People tend to think of grossly wicked people as if they were a distinct group, far removed from themselves. Indeed, the scripture say that **"Most men will proclaim each his own goodness, But who can find a faithful man?"** (Proverbs 20:6) Some years ago, a drug dealer boasted to me that he had never stolen anything in his life. And within a few weeks of that time, a habitual thief boasted to me that he had never sold drugs. The scriptures answer such claims by saying **"But they, measuring themselves by themselves, and comparing themselves among themselves, are not wise."** (2 Corinthians 10:12) And the passage before us answers it by saying, **"in whatever you judge another you condemn yourself; for you who judge practice the same things."**

But some will angrily answer, "What do you mean? I have never, even once, done anything even remotely like those things described in Romans 1." These people need to carefully consider the very words of Jesus Himself, when He said, **"You have heard that it was said to those of old, 'You shall not commit adultery.' But I say to you that whoever looks at a woman to lust for her has already committed adultery with her in his heart."** (Matthew 5:27-28)

Indeed, Jesus even went so far as to say, **"You have heard that it was said to those of old, 'You shall not murder, and whoever murders will be in danger of the judgment.' But I say to you that whoever is angry with his brother without a cause shall be in danger of the judgment."** (Matthew 5:21-22)

Why is this? **"For *the Lord does* not *see* as man sees; for man looks at the outward appearance, but the LORD looks at the heart."** (1 Samuel 16:7) And **"The heart *is* deceitful above all *things*, And desperately wicked; Who can know it?"** (Jeremiah 17:9) God further says that **"As in water face *reflects* face, So a man's heart *reveals* the man."** (Proverbs 27:19)

So, even though it may be true that we have never committed such-and-such a sin, that is immaterial. For in God's opinion, (and since He is the *ultimate* Judge, His opinion is the only one that counts,) our hearts are no different from the hearts of those who commit the gross wickedness described in Romans 1. And that is why He says **"in whatever you judge another you condemn yourself; for you who judge practice the same things."** Your sins may not be exactly the same as those sins, but they are the same in the essence of the heart. For who has never, even once, looked lustfully on someone to whom they are not married? And who has never become angry with their brother without just cause?

And that is why the next chapter goes on to apply this same condemnation to all, to everyone. So we read,

> **"What then? Are we better *than they*? Not at all. For we have previously charged both Jews and Greeks that they**

are all under sin. As it is written: *'There is none righteous, no, not one; There is none who understands; There is none who seeks after God. They have all turned aside; They have together become unprofitable; There is none who does good, no, not one.'"* (Romans 3:9-12)

We can never even begin to understand our spiritual condition, nor the justice of God's condemnation of ourselves, until we realize our guilt before God. For **"we are all like an unclean thing, And all our righteousnesses are like filthy rags."** (Isaiah 64:6) David prayed, **"Do not enter into judgment with Your servant, For in Your sight no one living is righteous."** (Psalm 143:2) So we have nothing to offer God, no plea of excuse, no reasoning to justify ourselves. We are all guilty. And we are not just "a little bit" guilty, or "sort of" guilty. We do not have "some good and some bad" to offer God, but rather **"the LORD saw that the wickedness of man *was* great in the earth, and *that* every intent of the thoughts of his heart *was* only evil continually."** (Genesis 6:5)

This understanding is, *of necessity*, the very first beginning of a relationship with God. If we think that God will accept any imagined merit we might offer Him, we are only deceiving ourselves. **"For by grace you have been saved through faith, and that not of yourselves;** *it is* **the gift of God, not of works, lest anyone should boast."** (Ephesians 2:8-9) Our relationship with Him either is based on unmerited pardon or it does not exist at all. For **"If we say that we have no sin, we deceive ourselves, and the truth is not in us."** (1 John 1:8) But **"the blood of Jesus Christ His Son cleanses us from all sin."** (1 John 1:7) And **"it is the blood *that* makes atonement for the soul."** (Leviticus 17:11) This blood was shed by our Lord Jesus Christ at Calvary two thousand years ago.

This is the offering that He has Himself provided. And it is the only offering that He will accept. And the only way to obtain a pardon is to simply believe what He has said about it. That is, through faith. And this is why we read that Abraham **"believed in the LORD, and He accounted it to him for righteousness."** (Genesis 15:6)

And that is why Romans 3 goes on to say,

> "But now the righteousness of God apart from the law is revealed, being witnessed by the Law and the Prophets, even the righteousness of God, through faith in Jesus Christ, to all and on all who believe. For there is no difference; for all have sinned and fall short of the glory of God, being justified freely by His grace through the redemption that is in Christ Jesus, whom God set forth *as* a propitiation by His blood, through faith, to demonstrate His righteousness, because in His forbearance God had passed over the sins that were previously committed, to demonstrate at the present time His righteousness, that He might be just and the justifier of the one who has faith in Jesus. Where *is* boasting then? It is excluded. By what law? Of works? No, but by the law of faith. Therefore we conclude that a man is justified by faith apart from the deeds of the law." (Romans 3:21-28)

This rather long passage is quoted as a block because it all stands together. The point is that God is righteous in justifying **"the one who has faith in Jesus."** It is pointed out that this is not a new concept, but that it was also **"witnessed by the Law and the Prophets,"** that is, in the Old Testament. And the great and all important conclusion is **"that a man is justified by faith apart from the deeds of the law."** (Romans 3:28)

It is impossible to overstress the importance of this great fact, **"that a man is justified by faith apart from the deeds of the law."** Aside from such foundation truths as the divinity of Jesus and the reliability of God's word, the Bible, there is no single truth more important than this. We are justified **"by faith,"** that is, by simply believing what God has said in His word, the Bible. And what we *do* has nothing to do with it. Indeed, the last chapter of Isaiah says that **"all our righteousnesses *are* like filthy rags."** (Isaiah 64:6) The translators have softened the language here, for the Hebrew word here translated *filthy* is a form of *'idda*. (word number 5708 in Strong's Hebrew dictionary) This word literally means *menstrous*. Here the Holy Spirit intentionally used an exceedingly disgusting word in describing His attitude about any good works we might offer Him. That is why He says, as we have already noticed, **"For by grace you have been saved through faith, and that not of yourselves; *it is* the gift of God, not of works, lest anyone should boast."** (Ephesians 2:8-9) And that is also why He says **"For God so loved the world that He gave His only begotten Son, that whoever believes in Him should not perish but have everlasting life."** (John 3:16)

After the great God of all the universe has made so great an offering as this for our salvation, what must He think of *any* and *every* attempt to seek some other means of His grace. He finds all such imaginations utterly disgusting! And they make Him exceedingly angry. He says

> **"Anyone who has rejected Moses' law dies without mercy on the testimony of two or three witnesses. Of how much worse punishment, do you suppose, will he be thought worthy who has trampled the Son of God underfoot, counted the blood of the covenant by which he was sanctified a common thing, and insulted the Spirit of grace? For we know Him who said, 'Vengeance is Mine, I will repay,' says the Lord. And again, 'The LORD will judge His people.' It is a fearful thing to fall into the hands of the living God."** (Hebrews 10:28-31)

Next, In Romans 4, the Holy Spirit takes up the example of Abraham, stressing that **"the promise that he would be the heir of the world *was* not to Abraham or to his seed through the law, but through the righteousness of faith."** (Romans 4:13) He then went on to explain, saying, **"For if those who are of the law *are* heirs, faith is made void and the promise made of no effect, because the law brings about wrath; for where there is no law *there is* no transgression."** (Romans 4:14-15)

We are spending so much time on this point, because that is what the Holy Spirit did. He did not just say this and leave it, but stressed it very strongly by saying it again and again, in various ways. Why did He do this? Because it would be difficult to find a single point more basic and central to the gospel. If this is lost (and sadly, it has been lost to a very large part of professing Christendom) the basic, central essence of the gospel, the very *root* of the Christian message, has been lost.

And this part of the message is concluded with the words, **"Therefore *it is* of faith that *it might be* according to grace, so that the promise might be sure to all the seed, not only to those who are of the law, but also to those who are of the faith of Abraham, who is the father of us all."** (Romans 4:16) So the reason for this is **"that the promise might be sure."**

This certainty of the promise, that is, the fact that it is both certain and sure, is an *essential* part of the gospel message. For the Bible is not a book of thinking, or of hoping, but of knowing. Indeed, a computer search of the translation we are using, (the NKJV) shows that the word **"know"** occurs 964 times and its form **"knowing"** 52 times, for a total of well over a thousand times, while the word **"think"** can be found only 59 times and its form **"thinking"** only 3 times, for a total of 62. So the word **"know"** occurs over sixteen times as often as the word **"think."**

But what does this confidence, this certainty, produce in the life of a believer? It produces peace, as we find when we move into Romans five.

> **"Therefore, having been justified by faith, we have peace with God through our Lord Jesus Christ, through whom also we have access by faith into this grace in which we stand, and rejoice in hope of the glory of God."** (Romans 5:1-2)

This **"peace with God"** is not simply a matter of God no longer being angry with us. Once we have indeed trusted in the blood Jesus shed at Calvary, that peace is a settled and unchangeable reality. Instead, this **"peace with God"** is a matter of *our* realizing that He is no longer angry with us, that we no longer have any reason to fear Him. As we read in 1 John 4:18, **"There is no fear in love; but perfect love casts out fear, because fear involves torment."** And the rest of this verse adds that **"he who fears has not been made perfect in love."**

So this **"peace with God"** is a peace on our side. Rather than a reference to the fact that God is no longer angry with us, it is a reference to *our understanding* of that fact. For this peace is the *necessary* result of any faith that actually saves. An old Christian hymn expresses this in the words:

> Oh! the peace for ever flowing
> From God's thoughts of His own Son,
> Oh, the peace of simply knowing
> On the cross that all was done.

But we need to notice that this peace is not the only result of this faith. For in Romans 5:2 we also see that it makes us **"rejoice in hope."** And this is not just some kind of a random hope, but a **"hope of the glory of God."** Nor is this an "I hope I pass the test" kind of a hope, but rather, the hope of a laborer as payday approaches. That is, a sure expectation of what is to come. He labors patiently all week, or all month, or whatever his pay period is, confident that his employer can be trusted to give him his promised pay on the due date. This confident **"hope of the glory of God"** produces joy in our hearts.

But this confident hope is far more than just a source of joy. For it is also **"an anchor of the soul, both sure and steadfast."** (Hebrews 6:19) This gives us power over our circumstances. When someone is asked how they are doing and they answer, "pretty good, under the circumstances," some habitually respond by asking, "What are you doing down there?" In the next few verses, the Holy Spirit expresses this thought by saying:

> **"And not only *that*, but we also glory in tribulations, knowing that tribulation produces perseverance; and perseverance, character; and character, hope. Now hope does not disappoint, because the love of God has been poured out in our hearts by the Holy Spirit who was given to us."** (Romans 5:3-5)

If this **"sure and steadfast"** hope is active in our hearts, even tribulation produces joy instead of sorrow. Why? Because we know that **"tribulation produces perseverance; and perseverance, character; and character, hope."** That is, we know that the very troubles that so sorely vex us, are nothing but the tools God is using to conform us to His image. So we can even rejoice in the very troubles that seek to wear us down. And this confidence, this **"sure and steadfast"** hope, **"does not disappoint, because the love of God has been poured out in our hearts by the Holy Spirit who was given to us."**

It all comes down to love, **"the love of God,"** **"in our hearts."** But as we noticed above, 1 John 4:18 ends with the words, **"he who fears has not been made perfect in love."** And now the Holy Spirit begins to deal with that fear by returning to the basic fundamentals of the gospel.

A concept that seems obvious to the natural mind is that we need to be "good enough" to go to heaven. But God says the very opposite. For Jesus said, **"I have not come to call the righteous, but sinners, to repentance."** (Luke 5:32) And the same Apostle, Paul, used by the Holy Spirit to give us the book of Romans, also wrote.

"This is a faithful saying and worthy of all acceptance, that Christ Jesus came into the world to save sinners, of whom I am chief. However, for this reason I obtained mercy, that in me first Jesus Christ might show all longsuffering, as a pattern to those who are going to believe on Him for everlasting life." (1 Timothy 1:15-16)

So in returning to the basic fundamentals of the gospel, the Holy Spirit, who is the real author of these words, began by saying:

> "For when we were still without strength, in due time Christ died for the ungodly. For scarcely for a righteous man will one die; yet perhaps for a good man someone would even dare to die. But God demonstrates His own love toward us, in that while we were still sinners, Christ died for us." (Romans 5:6-8)

Our confidence does not come from any imagination that we are good enough to be accepted by God, but from the fact that **"while we were still sinners, Christ died for us."**

Now comes a rather long explanation of the principle that salvation is not based on merit, but is a free gift.

> "Therefore, just as through one man sin entered the world, and death through sin, and thus death spread to all men, because all sinned-- (For until the law sin was in the world, but sin is not imputed when there is no law. Nevertheless death reigned from Adam to Moses, even over those who had not sinned according to the likeness of the transgression of Adam, who is a type of Him who was to come. But the free gift *is* not like the offense. For if by the one man's offense many died, much more the grace of God and the gift by the grace of the one Man, Jesus Christ, abounded to many. And the gift *is* not like *that which came* through the one who sinned. For the judgment *which came* from one *offense* resulted in condemnation, but the free gift *which came* from many offenses *resulted*

> in justification. For if by the one man's offense death reigned through the one, much more those who receive abundance of grace and of the gift of righteousness will reign in life through the One, Jesus Christ.) Therefore, as through one man's offense *judgment* came to all men, resulting in condemnation, even so through one Man's righteous act *the free gift came* to all men, resulting in justification of life." (Romans 5:12-18)

This concept, that salvation is a **"free gift,"** is inextricably linked with the fact that our **"hope"** is **"sure and steadfast,"** with our confidence that we can rest secure in the fact that our sins have been forgiven. Not that they *will be* forgiven, but that they *have been* forgiven.

That is, that this is a "done deal." We can therefore rest, simply rest, secure in the certain confidence that we will most definitely be with the Lord we so love, in His home in heaven. For if this confidence were based on any kind of imagined merit on our part, we could never be certain we were good enough. But when we realize that our salvation is a **"free gift,"** there remains no more room for doubt. This is finally summed up in the words:

> "For as by one man's disobedience many were made sinners, so also by one Man's obedience many will be made righteous. Moreover the law entered that the offense might abound. But where sin abounded, grace abounded much more, so that as sin reigned in death, even so grace might reign through righteousness to eternal life through Jesus Christ our Lord." (Romans 5:19-21)

It would be difficult to overstress the fact that this is the *central essence* of Christianity. We can believe everything surrounding this, and still not actually be *Christians*, still not be among the Lord's own. In short, still lost, and on the way to eternal damnation. For *real* Christians are those who have given up any and every notion that there is, or ever will be, any merit whatsoever in themselves, and have trusted *entirely* in the merit of Christ. This is the subject of the entire book of Galatians, in which the Holy Spirit led the Apostle Paul to say of some who denied this, that **"I have doubts about you."** (Galatians 4:20)

There are some who **"want to pervert the gospel of Christ."** (Galatians 1:7) These imagine that, having *been* saved by the grace of God, they must now *keep* saved by being faithful to Him. To these the apostle said, again speaking in the Holy Spirit, **"Are you so foolish? Having begun in the Spirit, are you now being made perfect by the flesh?"** (Galatians 3:3) Those who are under this delusion fail to realize that if this notion were correct, their salvation would depend on something *they* must do, instead of being based *entirely* on what Jesus already *did*. They think *they* must "hold on," failing to realize that they are **"kept by the power of God."** (1 Peter 1:5) **"For I know whom I have believed and am persuaded that <u>He is able to keep</u> what I have committed to Him until that Day."** (2 Timothy 1:12) If our salvation must be maintained by *our* strength, we are doomed. For we are weak and often fail. But it is not maintained by *our* strength, but by *His* strength.

But others **"want to pervert the gospel"** in a different way by twisting this truth of our sure and steadfast hope in Christ into a wicked doctrine that we can just "get saved," and then do whatever we want. These people make this doctrine out to be that, once we are "saved," we can just do anything, and everything be all right, because **"the blood of Jesus Christ cleanses us from all sin."** (1 John 1:7) So a doctrine which is clearly taught by the Holy Spirit is wrested into a wicked lie of Satan. But in answer to this perversion of His message of grace, which He knew would come, the Holy Spirit warns us in the next chapter, Romans six, that this is *not* a license to sin. Instead, we are to live holy lives. So we read:

> **"What shall we say then? Shall we continue in sin that grace may abound? Certainly not! How shall we who died to sin live any longer in it? Or do you not know that as many of us as were baptized into Christ Jesus were baptized into His death? Therefore we were buried with Him through baptism into death, that just as Christ was raised from the dead by the glory of the Father, even so we also should walk in newness of life."** (Romans 6:1-4)

The Holy Spirit, and not just the Apostle Paul, had just told us, in Romans 5:20, that **"where sin abounded, grace abounded much more."** So now He says **"What shall we say then? Shall we continue in sin that grace may abound?" This would seem like an obvious conclusion, if we were to look at things from an earthly point of view. But what does the Holy Spirit say about this idea? **"Certainly not! How shall we who died to sin live any longer in it?"** Those who come to such a conclusion as this, only prove that they have basically zero understanding of God's overall program, His basic plan. God's plan is not to gloss over sin, to pretend that it does not matter, to just accept anything and everything.

We must remember that God is not only the creator, but also the ruler, of the entire universe. And a ruler cannot tolerate rebellion. If He were to do so, all His authority would be gone. He would be demoting Himself, and abdicating his responsibility as the great and final Judge of the entire universe. For His rule is not only absolute. It is also just. And justice *cannot* overlook wrongdoing.

So sin cannot be overlooked, and cannot simply be ignored. *All* sin must be dealt with, in complete and total justice. And that is why our beloved Lord Jesus came into the world. Not to ignore sin, but to deal with it, once and for all, in total justice. He himself took the punishment we deserved, and now offers us a pardon based on what *He* did, not on what *we* do. But the purpose of this pardon is not to "let us off the hook," but to conform us to His image. To make us like Himself. So the Holy Spirit says,

> **"do you not know that as many of us as were baptized into Christ Jesus were baptized into His death? Therefore we were buried with Him through baptism into death, that just as Christ was raised from the dead by the glory of the Father, even so we also should walk in newness of life."** (Romans 6:3-5)

While it is indeed true that **"if righteousness *comes* through the law, then Christ died in vain."** (Galatians 2:21) it is also true that we have been called to **"walk in newness of life."** Because **"as many of us as were baptized into Christ Jesus were baptized into His death."** But why? **"That just as Christ was raised from the dead by the glory of the Father, even so we also should walk in newness of life."** So the Holy Spirit continues:

> "For if we have been united together in the likeness of His death, certainly we also shall be *in the likeness* of *His* resurrection, knowing this, that our old man was crucified with *Him,* that the body of sin might be done away with, that we should no longer be slaves of sin. For he who has died has been freed from sin." (Romans 6:5-7)

So we are free from the slavery of sin. Once a slave had died, his master could no longer make him do anything. Even so, in applying the death of Christ to ourselves, God has freed us from the slavery in which we had been held. So He goes on to say:

> "Now if we died with Christ, we believe that we shall also live with Him, knowing that Christ, having been raised from the dead, dies no more. Death no longer has dominion over Him. For *the death* that He died, He died to sin once for all; but *the life* that He lives, He lives to God. Likewise you also, reckon yourselves to be dead indeed to sin, but alive to God in Christ Jesus our Lord." (Romans 6:8-11)

Here, the Holy Spirit teaches us through the example of the death and resurrection of Christ. We are told that God **"made Him who knew no sin *to be* sin for us."** (2 Corinthians 5:21) And this is how the only One who **"knew no sin"** could die **"to sin."** But here the Holy Spirit uses this to teach us that we should **"reckon yourselves to be dead indeed to sin."** But that is not all He teaches us through this example. For, having **"died to sin,"** our Redeemer now **"Lives to God."** So we are taught, not only to **"reckon"** ourselves **"dead indeed to sin,"** but also to reckon ourselves **"alive to God."** But it is not just **"alive to God,"** but **"alive to God in Christ Jesus our Lord."**

And this leads us to the passage which is central to the message of the sixth chapter of Romans:

> "Therefore do not let sin reign in your mortal body, that you should obey it in its lusts. And do not present your members *as* instruments of unrighteousness to sin, but present yourselves to God as being alive from the dead, and your members *as* instruments of righteousness to God. For sin shall not

have dominion over you, for you are not under law but under grace."** (Romans 6:12-14)

The first part of this message is easy to understand We are not to **"let sin reign"** in our mortal bodies. And we are not to present our **"members *as* instruments of unrighteousness unto sin."** Instead, we are to present our members **"*as* instruments of righteousness to God."** There is nothing even partly difficult to understand about this. In short, we are told, "don't do that, do this"

The next chapter, Romans 7, takes up what happens when Christians, having realized their need to live a holy life, set out to live such a life. Some have very wrongly imagined that this is a description of normal Christian experience, even going so far as to say such things as "This was even the experience of the great Apostle Paul." Those who talk this way only demonstrate that they have never understood the central subject of these first eight chapters of the book of Romans. For in this entire series, the Holy Spirit is taking us through the normal development of a Christian, from his first realization of his guilt before God, to full maturity in Christ. And Romans 7 describes a part of that process. But even as crawling, though a normal part of the development of a baby, is not normal human behavior, so the striving of Romans 7, while a normal and perhaps even a necessary part of Christian training, is not normal Christian behavior. For we read: **"For we know that the law is spiritual, but I am carnal, sold under sin. For what I am doing, I do not understand. For what I will to do, that I do not practice; but what I hate, that I do."** (Romans 7:14-15) This one statement should make everyone realize that this is *not* a description of normal Christianity. For we read:

> **"And I, brethren, could not speak to you as to spiritual *people* but as to carnal, as to babes in Christ. I fed you with milk and not with solid food; for until now you were not able to receive it, and even now you are still not able; for you are still carnal. For where *there are* envy, strife, and divisions among you, are you not carnal and behaving like *mere* men?"** (1 Corinthians 3:1-3)

The Holy Spirit's usage of this word **"carnal"** is here being opposed to the word **"spiritual."** And He plainly tells us that **"carnal"**

Christians are called **"babes in Christ."** Thus we see that the **"carnal"** experience described in the last half of Romans 7 is the experience of **"babes in Christ."** So the experience described here, though a necessary part of a young Christian's learning process, is not normal Christian behavior, any more than crawling is normal behavior for anyone except a baby.

The struggle of this learning experience is described in the words,

> **"If, then, I do what I will not to do, I agree with the law that *it is* good. But now, *it is* no longer I who do it, but sin that dwells in me. For I know that in me (that is, in my flesh) nothing good dwells; for to will is present with me, but *how* to perform what is good I do not find. For the good that I will *to do,* I do not do; but the evil I will not *to do,* that I practice."** (Romans 7:14-19)

There is something seriously wrong with anyone who claims to have been saved for more than a very little while, and has never had this experience. For anyone and everyone who has never experienced this struggle, has never made a serious attempt to actually follow and serve their Lord. Now this statement, after what I just said, may startle some. But that would only be those that did not notice what I actually said. While I said, and insist, that this is not *normal* Christian experience, I also said it is a normal part of Christian learning. As such, it is a *normal* part of their past experience, but it is *not* the present experience of *any* mature Christian. Anyone who is still experiencing this struggle is not mature in Christ.

The next section presents the beginning of an understanding of what is happening inside ourselves, as this learning process continues.

> **"Now if I do what I will not *to do,* it is no longer I who do it, but sin that dwells in me. I find then a law, that evil is present with me, the one who wills to do good. For I delight in the law of God according to the inward man. But I see another law in my members, warring against the law of my mind, and bringing me into captivity to the law of sin which is in my members."** (Romans 7:20-23)

Here, the Christian is beginning to understand what is happening. There are two opposing forces at work in his mind. There is a part of himself that really desires to do what is right, and what is good. But there is another part that does not care about God, or about others. That part, which is present in *all* of us, wars against the part that desires to be righteous, causing internal struggle. Our Lord mentioned this struggle, and its eventual outcome, when He said, **"Blessed are those who hunger and thirst for righteousness, For they shall be filled."** (Matthew 5:6)

This promise is not made to those who desire to *look* righteous, or to those who desire to *be considered* righteous, but rather to those who feel a deep, strong, internal desire (here called **"hunger and thirst"**) to actually *be* righteous. And what is the promise? **"They shall be filled."** How precious is this promise to those locked in the throes of this battle. During the seven very long years during which I personally passed trough this struggle, this was a continual comfort. To *know*, not to *think*, or to *hope*, but to *know*, that a blessed day was coming, in which I would be filled with righteousness! This kept me going, as I struggled from day to day.

But where does this struggle lead, in the life of a Christian? It finally leads to a crash. To a time when the Christian finally throws up his hands in despair, and cries out:

> **"O wretched man that I am! Who will deliver me from this body of death?"** (Romans 7:24)

Many years ago, I heard this described on the radio by the great Charles Swindoll, who later became the Chancellor of Dallas Theological Seminary. He said that when a man is first saved, he starts out to serve Jesus, and, filled with the joy of the Lord, he says, "Man, this is easy." Then the struggle begins, and after a while he shakes his head, and says, "Man, this is hard." Then Satan notices him and the struggle *really* begins. And after a time he throws up his hands and says, "Man, this is *impossible!*" Swindoll then paused in his inimitable way, and said, "*Now*, you're starting to get somewhere."

Brother Swindoll was stressing the lesson that this experience is designed to teach us all. This is a lesson that we can *only* learn by experience. That, although we are called to live a righteous life, *we* simply *cannot* do it. Of course, I have intentionally stressed the word "*we*." For this can indeed be done. And it not only *can*, but it *must* be done. But *each* of us needs to understand that he, or she, *cannot* do this. It can *only* be done by the Holy Spirit, who indwells every person that has truly trusted in the Lord Jesus Christ, and Him alone, for the salvation of their souls.

But now we come to a sudden burst of understanding:

> **"I thank God--through Jesus Christ our Lord! So then, with the mind I myself serve the law of God, but with the flesh the law of sin."** (Romans 7:25)

So now, suddenly, the Christian realizes a great truth. That the mind and the flesh are two different things. My mind, that is, the *real* me, the deep desire of my heart, serves God. But my flesh is weak, and is often tripped up by sin. And all of us, even the most mature Christians among us, are often tripped up by sin, **"For we all stumble in many things."** (James 3:2) And even the great Apostle Paul had to say, **"I know nothing against myself, yet I am not justified by this; but He who judges me is the Lord."** (1 Corinthians 4:4)

And this realization, that even though my flesh still serves the law of sin, my mind, that is, the real me, serves the law of God, leads to a full comprehension of our standing in Christ. So Romans 8 begins with the words:

> **"*There is* therefore now no condemnation to those who are in Christ Jesus, who do not walk according to the flesh, but according to the Spirit. For the law of the Spirit of life in Christ Jesus has made me free from the law of sin and death. For what the law could not do in that it was weak through the flesh, God *did* by sending His own Son in the likeness of sinful flesh, on account of sin: He condemned sin in the flesh, that the righteous requirement of the law might be fulfilled in us who do not walk according to the flesh but according to the Spirit."** (Romans 7:25-8:4)

This is celebrated in the following words from another old hymn:

> "No condemnation!" — precious word!
> Consider it, my soul!
> Thy sins were all on Jesus laid;
> His stripes have made thee whole.
>
> "No condemnation!" — O my soul,
> 'Tis God that speaks the word,
> Perfect in comeliness art thou
> In Christ, the risen Lord.

So that is why the Holy Spirit says,

> "*There is* therefore now no condemnation to those who are in Christ Jesus, who do not walk according to the flesh, but according to the Spirit. For the law of the Spirit of life in Christ Jesus has made me free from the law of sin and death. For what the law could not do in that it was weak through the flesh, God *did* by sending His own Son in the likeness of sinful flesh, on account of sin: He condemned sin in the flesh, that the righteous requirement of the law might be fulfilled in us who do not walk according to the flesh but according to the Spirit." (Romans 8:1-4)

Until our hearts get hold of this precious truth that there is no longer any condemnation for us, we can never even begin to reach real maturity in Christ. But it is not *only* true that there is no condemnation for us. Rather, we are **"free from the law of sin and death."** Sin is not ignored, in us or in anyone else. Rather, it is condemned, in the very act that won our justification. Sin, our sin, was condemned at Calvary, and now we are free. So now **"the righteous requirement of the law"** is fulfilled in us who **"do not walk according to the flesh but according to the Spirit."**

Next we find the great secret of life in Christ.

> "**For those who live according to the flesh set their minds on the things of the flesh, but those *who live* according to the Spirit, the things of the Spirit. For to be carnally minded *is* death, but to be spiritually minded *is* life and peace. Because the carnal mind *is* enmity against God; for it is not subject to the law of God, nor indeed can be. So then, those who are in the flesh cannot please God. But you are not in the flesh but in the Spirit, if indeed the Spirit of God dwells in you. Now if anyone does not have the Spirit of Christ, he is not His. And if Christ *is* in you, the body *is* dead because of sin, but the Spirit *is* life because of righteousness."** (Romans 8:5-10)

The carnal mind **"is not subject to the law of God, nor indeed can be."** It is not simply that the carnal mind does not *wish* to submit to the law of God. No, it is far more than that. Rather, the carnal mind is not *capable* of submitting to the law of God. Such submission is simply not in its nature. It is incapable of such submission. That is why we must give up the carnal mind. As long as that mind is active in us, we remain in the state described in the last chapter. **"For the good that I will *to do*, I do not do; but the evil I will not *to do*, that I practice."** (Romans 7:19)

The Holy Spirit continues by saying,

> "**But if the Spirit of Him who raised Jesus from the dead dwells in you, He who raised Christ from the dead will also give life to your mortal bodies through His Spirit who dwells in you. Therefore, brethren, we are debtors--not to the flesh, to live according to the flesh. For if you live according to the flesh you will die; but if by the Spirit you put to death the deeds of the body, you will live."** (Romans 8:11-13)

To really understand this, we must now return to a passage from chapter six that we previously treated only in part. That passage was,

> "**For if we have been united together in the likeness of His death, certainly we also shall be *in the likeness* of *His* resurrection, knowing this, that our old man was crucified with *Him*, that the body of sin might be done away with, that we should

no longer be slaves of sin. For he who has died has been freed from sin. Now if we died with Christ, we believe that we shall also live with Him, knowing that Christ, having been raised from the dead, dies no more. Death no longer has dominion over Him. For *the death* that He died, He died to sin once for all; but *the life* that He lives, He lives to God. Likewise you also, reckon yourselves to be dead indeed to sin, but alive to God in Christ Jesus our Lord." (Romans 6:5-11)

It took me many years to understand this passage. For a false interpretation of its meaning had become ingrained in my mind. I understood the falsehood of the conclusion resulting from my interpretation. But for many years I could not find where the problem lay. How often does this happen to all of us. We make an assumption about the meaning of something God said, and our minds tell us that this notion is what God said. But this always leads us into error. Sometimes the error is small, and sometimes it is very large, but it is always error. We need to draw a clear line between what God said, and what we think that means. For what God said is always right. But sadly, what we think that means, is often wrong, and sometimes quite wrong.

In this case, I had assumed that the words **"reckon yourselves to be dead indeed to sin,"** meant "reckon yourself dead indeed to the power of sin to tempt you." And in *that* sense I was distressingly conscious that I was *not* dead to sin. I hated sin, but, regardless of how much I hated it, I fell into it every day. It seemed that almost every time temptation came, I fell into it. And so I kept saying to myself, "But I am *not* dead to sin." And *that* sense I indeed was not dead to sin, and still am not dead to sin, even after seventy-five years of following Christ.

But one night, after many years, I casually picked up a book that I had never read, and opened it at random. I looked at a page and my eyes fell on the words, " 'reckon ye also yourselves to be dead indeed unto sin, but alive unto God through Jesus Christ our Lord.' This means we should not be walking around with a sense of condemnation." Suddenly it hit me like a thunderbolt. *Dead to the power of sin to condemn me!*

In a moment's time, I was delivered. The book, whose title I do not remember, fell from my hands. I grabbed up my Bible, and read over many of the great and wonderful promises contained in it. I started in the gospel of John, **"Most assuredly, I say to you, he who hears My word and believes in Him who sent Me has everlasting life, and shall not come into judgment, but has passed from death into life."** (John 5:24) and ended up in Romans 8, where I read that wonderful passage beginning

> "What then shall we say to these things? If God *is* for us, who *can be* against us? He who did not spare His own Son, but delivered Him up for us all, how shall He not with Him also freely give us all things? Who shall bring a charge against God's elect? *It is* God who justifies. Who *is* he who condemns? *It is* Christ who died, and furthermore is also risen, who is even at the right hand of God, who also makes intercession for us." (Romans 8:31-34)

When I finished this passage I physically collapsed, and lay there laughing like a madman. Yes, I had sinned. Yes, I was guilty. But my God had pardoned me, and would no longer accept any charges against me. Why? Because I deserved it? *No*, in no way. But because, and *only* because Jesus had died - for me! For miserable, guilty *me*! And I was free, pardoned, and accepted before the throne of the *almighty God*!

Suddenly I could now understand the next words of this passage which had so long perplexed me.

> "Therefore do not let sin reign in your mortal body, that you should obey it in its lusts. And do not present your members *as* instruments of unrighteousness to sin, but present yourselves to God as being alive from the dead, and your members *as* instruments of righteousness to God. For sin shall not have dominion over you, for you are not under law but under grace." (Romans 6:5-14)

I had long noticed the words **"do not let sin reign... that you should obey it."** And I had simply missed the rest of this all important message. These words are indeed there, and are indeed important. But few seem to understand them. It says **"For sin shall not have dominion over you, for you are not under law but under grace."**

Here, the Holy Spirit has not told us that sin *should* not have dominion over us, but that it *shall* not have dominion over us. This is not a command. Nor is it advice. Instead of either of these, it is the declaration of a *fact*. The God of heaven has declared that sin *shall not* have dominion over you. This is something that is already in effect, and shall be forever. The power of sin in our lives *has been broken*. It would be difficult to overstress this fact. But the Holy Spirit's explanation of this is **"for you are not under law, but under grace."** This is a *basic* and *fundamental* part of the gospel of Jesus Christ. And any denial of this great truth is a departure from that gospel. And that does not mean just a departure from some details of the gospel, but from its *central message*. For we are not saved just so we can go to heaven, but **"*to be* conformed to the image of"** the Son of God. (Romans 8:30) And being **"conformed to his image"** absolutely requires that we be set free from sin.

But the Holy Spirit continues by saying,

> **"What then? Shall we sin because we are not under law but under grace? Certainly not! Do you not know that to whom you present yourselves slaves to obey, you are that one's slaves whom you obey, whether of sin *leading* to death, or of obedience *leading* to righteousnes?"** (Romans 6:15-16)

Why make yourself a slave, when you are free? But if you choose to obey the dictates of sin, you are presenting yourself as a slave to sin. So the Holy Spirit continues.

> **"For when you were slaves of sin, you were free in regard to righteousness. What fruit did you have then in the things of which you are now ashamed? For the end of those things *is* death. But now having been set free from sin, and having become slaves of God, you have your fruit to holiness, and the end, everlasting life."** (Romans 6:20-22)

In this passage, God is not saying that the power of sin is not real. Nor is He saying that sin has no power to enslave. Indeed, in another place He speaks of some, that they **"cannot cease from sin."** (2 Peter 2:14) But for those who have truly trusted in the Lord Jesus Christ, **"sin shall not have dominion over"** them. And they have **"been set free**

from sin." They have now become willing **"slaves of God,"** and now produce **"fruit to holiness."** And their end is **"everlasting life."**

The Holy Spirit continues this message with that great declaration, **"For the wages of sin *is* death, but the gift of God *is* eternal life in Christ Jesus our Lord."** (Romans 6:23) But we need to notice that this **"eternal life"** is a **"gift,"** not **"wages."** The only **"wages"** paid by God are **"the wages of sin,"** which is **"death."** Our entire life, our entire being, rests on this great fact, that our salvation is not based on merit, but is a **"free gift."** (Romans 5:16)

We need to understand that we can no more deserve to *stay* saved than we did to *be* saved in the first place. And staying saved, we can no more deserve God's favor *now*, than we could *before* we trusted in Christ. *All* is based, *always and forever*, on the precious blood that our Lord Jesus shed for us at Calvary. Nothing less, and nothing more. Our acceptance is based *entirely* on the blood. And that is why it is reliable. For our spiritual states change from day to day, and even from moment to moment. For one moment we can be rejoicing in the love of our Savior, and the next moment, we can turn to sinful thoughts. But the sacrifice of the precious blood of Christ never changes. It is *always* there, and it *always* avails. And that is why we are *always* accepted, once we have indeed trusted in that blood, and in nothing else.

We remember that 1 Corinthians 15:56 says, **"The sting of death *is* sin, and the strength of sin *is* the law."** And herein lies the secret to understanding the victorious Christian life. For **"Christ has redeemed us from the curse of the law, having become a curse for us (for it is written, 'Cursed is everyone who hangs on a tree')."** (Galatians 3:13) And that is how we have become dead to sin. For, as we are told in Romans 7:4, we **"have become dead to the law."** Our wonderful Lord, Jesus Christ, **"became a curse for us,"** to redeem us **"from the curse of the law."** And now **"the strength of sin,"** which is **"the law,"** has been broken, because our Lord took the curse of that law upon himself. So now the law can no longer condemn us, and the power of sin is broken.

We remember that when mankind committed their first sin, **"they heard the sound of the LORD God walking in the garden,"** and they **"hid themselves from the presence of the LORD God."** (Genesis 3:8) Even so, guilt on our hearts makes us shrink from the face of **"He who is holy, He who is true."** (Revelation 3:2) But when we realize that *everything*, even our *present* acceptance before him is based *entirely* on the blood of Christ, our fear vanishes. We confess our sin, and **"He is faithful and just to forgive us *our* sins"** and not only to forgive us, but also **"to cleanse us from all unrighteousness."** (1 John 1:9) Thus, then, is brought to pass the fact that **"There is no fear in love; but perfect love casts out fear."** (1 John 4:18) When we realize that we *have been* forgiven, that we *are* accepted, and that both of these are fixed, unchangeable, and permanent, our fear disappears. We come back to Him, confess our sin, and rejoice in His love.

It is this confidence that gives us the power to actually live holy lives. For rejoicing in this confidence restores our hearts to Himself, and puts us **"in the Spirit."** And we are explicitly told that this is how we actually live out the holy life. For we read:

> **"I say then: Walk in the Spirit, and you shall not fulfill the lust of the flesh. For the flesh lusts against the Spirit, and the Spirit against the flesh; and these are contrary to one another, so that you do not do the things that you wish. But if you are led by the Spirit, you are not under the law. Now the works of the flesh are evident, which are: adultery, fornication, uncleanness, lewdness, idolatry, sorcery, hatred, contentions, jealousies, outbursts of wrath, selfish ambitions, dissensions, heresies, envy, murders, drunkenness, revelries, and the like; of which I tell you beforehand, just as I also told *you* in time past, that those who practice such things will not inherit the kingdom of God. But the fruit of the Spirit is love, joy, peace, longsuffering, kindness, goodness, faithfulness, gentleness, self-control. Against such there is no law. And those *who are* Christ's have crucified the flesh with its passions and desires. If we live in the Spirit, let us also walk in the Spirit."** (Galatians 5:16-25)

We noticed earlier that Romans 8:7 teaches us that the carnal mind is not *capable* of submitting to the law of God, and not simply that the carnal mind does not *wish* to submit to the law of God. That is, that such a walk is not in its nature. But here we see that if we **"walk in the Spirit,"** we will practice **"love, joy, peace, longsuffering, kindness, goodness, faithfulness, gentleness,"** and **"self-control."** Now most Christians get this backwards.

They imagine that this scripture teaches that if we are doing all these things we will be walking **"in the Spirit."** but that is not what it says. Rather, it says that these things will be **"the fruit of"** walking **"in the Spirit."** Even as **"the carnal mind"** is incapable of submitting to the law of God, **"the Spirit,"** that is, the new nature, which is in every real Christian, never sins. For, even as submission to God is not in the carnal nature, sin, that is, any kind of rebellion against God, is not in the new nature.

This shows us that "trying to do good" is an old nature activity. The new nature does not *try* to be good. It *is* good. The old nature wants to look good. So it tries to be good. But it cannot. The new nature, on the other hand, never sins. So it never *tries* to do good. That is simply its *nature*. A little girl cannot be a little boy, and a little boy cannot be a little girl. They simply have two different natures, and neither can ever be the other, no matter how hard they might try. Even so, the old nature, **"the carnal mind"** cannot do good, and the new nature, **"the Spirit,"** never sins.

So, although the words sound shocking, the hard truth is that we need to *stop* trying to be good. Just stop it. We cannot do it, not even one of us. So just stop trying. But there is a way to do good. And that is to walk in the Spirit. And as long as we are walking **"in the Spirit"** we will never sin. Not even once. And not even a little bit. For even as goodness in not in the nature of **"the carnal mind,"** so sin is not in the nature of **"the Spirit."**

That may be all well and good, but how do we do that? *How* do we **"walk in the Spirit"**? We have seen that it is not by trying to do good. Instead, we need to get our minds off ourselves entirely, and set them upon our wonderful Savior! As long as our entire hearts, minds, and beings, are simply consumed by His love, we will be **"in the Spirit,"** and we will live *absolutely* holy lives, without even trying. It will simply be our nature. And *that* is the secret of a mature Christian life.

This concentration upon our Savior, who He is, and What He has done for us, fills us with confidence. And this confidence removes all fear. We realize that we now have become **"children of God,"** and this is not just something that *will be*, but something that has *already* happened. It is a done deal, as we are told:

> "For as many as are led by the Spirit of God, these are sons of God. For you did not receive the spirit of bondage again to fear, but you received the Spirit of adoption by whom we cry out, "Abba, Father." The Spirit Himself bears witness with our spirit that we are children of God, and if children, then heirs--heirs of God and joint heirs with Christ, if indeed we suffer with *Him*, that we may also be glorified together." (Romans 8:14-17)

This knowledge, that we have already become **"children of God,"** and that we are, even now, **"joint heirs with Christ,"** makes us realize that the **"sufferings of this present time"** are trivial. They are not even worthy to be compared with **"the glory which shall be revealed in us."** And this leaves us eager for what is coming, as described by the Holy Spirit in the following words:

> "For I consider that the sufferings of this present time are not worthy *to be compared* with the glory which shall be revealed in us. For the earnest expectation of the creation eagerly waits for the revealing of the sons of God. For the creation was subjected to futility, not willingly, but because of Him who subjected *it* in hope; because the creation itself also will be delivered from the bondage of corruption into the glorious liberty of the children of God. For we know that the whole creation groans and labors with birth pangs together until now. Not only *that*, but we also who have the firstfruits of the Spirit, even we ourselves groan within ourselves, eagerly waiting for the adoption, the redemption of our body." (Romans 8:18-23)

Next, the Holy Spirit stresses this hope, saying:

> "For we were saved in this hope, but hope that is seen is not hope; for why does one still hope for what he sees? But if we hope for what we do not see, we eagerly wait for *it* with perseverance. the Spirit also helps in our weaknesses. For we do not know what we should pray for as we ought, but the Spirit Himself makes intercession for us with groanings which cannot be uttered." (Romans 8:24-26)

And all this is finally summed up in that great passage whose force caused me to physically collapse on the night it finally hit me. I literally lay there, laughing like a madman. And when this really gets hold of others, it will have a similar effect upon them.

"What then shall we say to these things? If God *is* for us, who *can be* against us? He who did not spare His own Son, but delivered Him up for us all, how shall He not with Him also freely give us all things? Who shall bring a charge against God's elect? *It is* God who justifies. Who *is* he who condemns? *It is* Christ who died, and furthermore is also risen, who is even at the right hand of God, who also makes intercession for us. Who shall separate us from the love of Christ? *Shall* tribulation, or distress, or persecution, or famine, or nakedness, or peril, or sword? As it is written: *'For Your sake we are killed all day long; We are accounted as sheep for the slaughter.'* Yet in all these things we are more than conquerors through Him who loved us. For I am persuaded that neither death nor life, nor angels nor principalities nor powers, nor things present nor things to come, nor height nor depth, nor any other created thing, shall be able to separate us from the love of God which is in Christ Jesus our Lord." (Romans 8:31-39)

Before the night this got hold of me, I had always been what they call "a faithful witness." I continually presented the gospel to anyone and everyone who would listen, day after day, week after week, month after month, for years on end. And when I occasionally saw two people come to the Lord in a single year, I considered it a good year. But that night, everything changed. I suddenly began to see someone come to the Lord almost every day, and sometimes as many as six in one day!

That happened well over forty years ago. And since that day, I have found a fixed rule in my life. When my heart is full of Jesus, I am a twelve foot tall spiritual giant. And when my heart is full of anything else, I am just an old cripple. And it does not matter what that something else might be. It does not have to be something obviously sinful. It can just as well be money, respect, possessions, politics, or even just amusement. If my heart is not full of Christ, it is simply waste and empty. But as long as my heart is filled with Christ, my whole life is fruitful and prosperous. *This* is the secret of Christian maturity. And this understanding is the end goal of this eight chapter section of the book of Romans.

SECTION 2

CHAPTERS 9-11

God's Reliability

We need to consider this section of the epistle to the Romans in greater detail than the last section because it has been so severely wrested by many that claim to be teachers of the word of God. These false teachers insist that the ancient nation of Israel has been completely and permanently rejected by God. They imagine that the New Testament teaches that all the blessings promised to Israel in the Old Testament have been transferred to the church. And they claim that these three chapters support this idea. But in actual fact, they clearly teach the very opposite. This is critical to the message of this epistle, and indeed, to the entire message of the whole Bible, because it concerns the trustworthiness of God.

For while the overall presentation of the first eight chapters of this epistle has been the normal development of a Christian. The full maturity attained in this process is a complete confidence in the absolute reliability of the promises God has given us. And thus, this next three chapter section is actually a continuation of that same message. For, contrary to the evil message of the false teachers, if God cold justly break His promises to Israel, he cold fully as justly break the promises He made to us. If God could justly tell Israel, "I did not really mean you. I was actually speaking of a different group of people," He could fully as justly tell us, "I did not really mean you, I was actually speaking of a different group of people." Thus, if the ancient promises made by God to Israel are not inviolate, that is, if they are not absolutely reliable, then the promises made to ourselves are also not inviolate. If God is not going to actually fulfill the ancient promises He made to Israel, if He is not going to actually bring that ancient nation back to its ancient homeland and bless it there, then we have zero basis for our faith. For our *only* hope, the *only* basis for our faith, is that the promises made by God are *absolutely* reliable. If our God will not *actually* keep *every* promise He *ever* made, then we have *nothing*. In that case our faith would be based on a lie. And we would be suffering under a delusion. Thus we see that the doctrine that God has completely and permanently rejected Israel is not just an error in detail. Instead, it is a Satanic attack upon the very foundation of our faith. That is, it is not only false, but it is false at a *fundamental* level.

This important section of the word of God begins

> "I tell the truth in Christ, I am not lying, my conscience also bearing me witness in the Holy Spirit, that I have great sorrow and continual grief in my heart. For I could wish that I myself were accursed from Christ for my brethren, my countrymen according to the flesh, who are Israelites, to whom *pertain* the adoption, the glory, the covenants, the giving of the law, the service *of God,* and the promises; of whom *are* the fathers and from whom, according to the flesh, Christ came, who is over all, *the* eternally blessed God. Amen" (Romans 9:1-5)

Here the Apostle's great stress is his personal concern for his **"countrymen according to the flesh, who are Israelites."** But in considering these words, we need to remember that, although we are reading words written by a man, we are actually reading words that come from the Holy Spirit. Before we can fully understand what the Holy Spirit is here saying, we need to clearly understand who these words are written about. The object of these words is **"my countrymen according to the flesh, who are Israelites."** Thus we see that the object of the Apostle's concern (but actually, the Holy Spirit's concern) is unquestionably those who are Israelites **"according to the flesh."** That is, members of the *fleshly* nation of Israel. These words leave no chance whatsoever that the group he is talking about is actually the church. The specific words used here by the Holy Spirit completely eliminate that possibility.

But what does God say about these people? He explicitly says **"to whom *pertain* the adoption, the glory, the covenants, the giving of the law, the service *of God*, and the promises."** As we have already noticed, the words **"my countrymen according to the flesh, who are Israelites,"** just before these words, prove beyond a possibility of rational debate, that this is about those who are members of the *fleshly* nation of Israel. So here the Holy Spirit, speaking through Paul, has given us a list of things that *"pertain"* to the fleshly nation of Israel. This list is:

>"to whom *pertain*[2]
>
>the adoption,
>
>the glory,
>
>the covenants,
>
>the giving of the law,
>
>the service *of God*,
>
>and the promises."

It is critical to understand that the Holy Spirit is *not* here saying that these things pertain to (or belong to) the church. Rather, He expressly says that these things *"pertain"* to (or belong to) Paul's **"countrymen according to the flesh, who are Israelites."**

While everything in this list is important, for our present purposes we need to notice two specific items in this list. At the time this

---

2   Some may challenge this stress on the words **"to whom *pertain*,"** because the word pertain was not actually in the Greek text, but was added by the translators to complete the meaning. That is why the NKJV, which we are using, put this word in italics. But while this word was not actually in the Greek text, essentially every translation agrees that this is the true meaning of the Greek words actually used. The KJV gives exactly the same reading, while the ESV, the ISV, the NRSV and the HCSB all say *to them belong*, as does the MANT except it changes the word *belong* to *belongs*. The NASB says to *whom belongs*, as does the Douay, except that it says *belongeth*. Young's literal translation says *whose are*, which Darby also said, but he bracketed the word *are*. The CEV and the GWN use *is theirs*. The ASV gives *whose is*, while The NCV gives *they have*.

was written, **"the covenants"** and **"the promises"** still pertained to (or belonged to) Paul's **"countrymen according to the flesh, who are Israelites."** This was written long after Jesus had said, **"your house is left to you desolate,"** (Matthew 23:38 and Luke 13:35) long after Jesus had been crucified, long after that day of Pentecost when the Holy Spirit descended on the church, and long after Stephen had been stoned, completing Israel's rejection of Jesus as their Messiah. Yet **"the covenants"** and **"the promises"** still pertained to (or belonged to) the fleshly nation of Israel. This conclusively proves that at the time the Holy Spirit inspired Paul to write this epistle to the Romans, **"the covenants"** and **"the promises"** had not been transferred to the church. They still pertained to (or belonged to) the *fleshly* nation of Israel.

We now need to take a detailed look at the next verse. Romans 9:6 says, **"But it is not that the word of God has taken no effect. For they *are* not all Israel who *are* of Israel,"** We need to examine the last portion of this in the Greek. The Greek words translated **"For they *are* not all Israel who *are* of Israel"** are *"ου γαρ παντες οι εξ ισραηλ ουτοι ισραηλ."* (In our alphabet, *"ou gar pantes ho ex israel outoi israel"*) These Greek words translate literally to *"not for the out of Israel these Israel."* We need to carefully notice the words *"not ... the out of Israel these Israel."* Some think that these words mean that the true Israel is something different from "the out of Israel." If these words were taken *by themselves*, they could indeed be interpreted that way. But that is not the only possible interpretation of these words, even if taken only by themselves. They can fully as legitimately be interpreted to mean that *not every one out of Israel is Israel.* That is, that just being an Israelite by birth does not make someone a true Israelite. In order to determine which of these possible interpretations of this clause is correct, we need to consider what the rest of this passage says.

The true meaning of these words is clearly shown in the next verse, for Romans 9:7 says, **"nor *are they* all children because they are the seed of Abraham; but, 'In Isaac your seed shall be called.'"**

This statement has two parts, which we must examine separately. The first part is **"nor *are they* all children because they are the seed of Abraham."** The actual Greek words used here are *"ουδ οτι εισιν σπερμα αβρααμ παντες τεκνα"* (in our alphabet *"oud hoti eisin operma abraam pantes tekna."*) These Greek words translate literally to *"not however that* *am seed Abraham all children."* We need to particularly notice the Greek words ουδ (*oud*) and παντες (*pantes*.) These translate literally to *not* and *all*. So we see that individual words that literally mean *not* and *all* were explicitly used in the Greek text. This, then, clearly shows the meaning of the previous sentence. It was most certainly not that the *true* Israel was something different from the *physical* descendants of Abraham. Instead, this passage was *clearly* saying that just being a *physical* descendant of Abraham did not, in itself, make someone a *true* Israelite.

This is the same concept as what we see in John 1:47, where **"Jesus saw Nathanael coming toward Him, and said of him, 'Behold, an Israelite indeed, in whom is no deceit!'"** Here Jesus was saying that the fact that there was no deceit in Nathanel made him a *true* Israelite. And the Holy Spirit said through Paul that not every one "out of" Israel is an Israelite. The principle expressed in both passages is the same.

The second part of the statement we are considering is **"but, 'In Isaac your seed shall be called.'"** This is a direct quotation from Genesis 21:9-13, where we read,

> **"And Sarah saw the son of Hagar the Egyptian, whom she had borne to Abraham, scoffing. Therefore she said to Abraham, 'Cast out this bondwoman and her son; for the son of this bondwoman shall not be heir with my son,** *namely* **with Isaac.' And the matter was very displeasing in Abraham's sight because of his son.**
>
> **"But God said to Abraham, 'Do not let it be displeasing in your sight because of the lad or because of your bondwoman. Whatever Sarah has said to you, listen to her voice; for in Isaac your seed shall be called. Yet I will also make a nation of the son of the bondwoman, because he** *is* **your seed.'"**

Here God explicitly recognized that Ishmael was physically of the seed of Abraham, but said that he would not be counted as Abraham's seed. Thus, the example the Holy Spirit used here was *not* a case of substituting someone of faith (Abraham's spiritual seed) for Abraham's physical seed. It was rather a case of recognizing *some*, but not *all*, of Abraham's physical seed as being actually his "seed." This again shows that the Greek words which translate literally to *"not for the out of Israel these Israel."* Do not mean that the real Israel is something different from the physical descendants of Abraham. Rather, they mean that *just* being a physical descendant of Abraham does not make someone a *true* Israelite.

This leads us into the next statement, where in Romans 9:8 we read, **"That is, those who *are* the children of the flesh, these *are* not the children of God; but the children of the promise are counted as the seed."** Some imagine that while the words **"the children of the flesh"** clearly mean the physical descendants of Abraham, the words **"the children of promise"** mean the church. But this is an explanation of the meaning of the previous words. And we have just seen that those words mean that only *some* of the physical descendants of Abraham are counted as his *seed*. This sentence explains which of Abraham's physical descendants will be counted as his seed. Not all of Abraham's physical descendants are his "seed," but only the ones to whom the promise applied.

The Holy Spirit continues, **"For this *is* the word of promise: 'At this time I will come and Sarah shall have a son.'"** (Romans 9:9) The promise was that **"*Sarah*"** would have a son. And only the son of promise was counted as Abraham's seed. Now Sarah's son is not the church. Sarah's son was Isaac, and there is no passage anywhere in the Bible that can even be imagined to mean that the church was ever called Isaac. So the promised son the Holy Spirit was referring to was Isaac, a physical son of Abraham, and not the church.

We see this again in the next example the Holy Spirit gave us. For we read in Romans 9:10-12,

> **"And not only *this*, but when Rebecca also had conceived by one man, *even* by our father Isaac (for *the children* not yet being born, nor having done any good or evil, that the purpose of God according to election might stand, not of works but of Him who calls), it was said to her, 'The older shall serve the younger.' As it is written, 'Jacob I have loved, but Esau I have hated.'"**

There is not even one scripture that ever even hints at the idea that the church is Esau's younger brother, nor does any scripture whatsoever associate the name Jacob with the church. So we see that neither of these two examples of God's election speak of the church. They both speak of God choosing *some* of the *physical* seed of Abraham, but not *all* of it.

Next, we read

> **"What shall we say then?** *Is there* **unrighteousness with God? Certainly not! For He says to Moses, 'I will have mercy on whomever I will have mercy, and I will have compassion on whomever I will have compassion.' So then it is not of him who wills, nor of him who runs, but of God who shows mercy."** (Romans 9:14-16)

This passage is critically important to coming to an understanding of what God is saying, particularly when considered in the light of the preceding one.

In verses 10-12, the Holy Spirit stressed that He made the choice between Jacob and Esau before they had done **"any good or evil."** Now we are told that **"***it is* **not of him who wills, nor of him who runs, but of God who shows mercy."** Why is this so important to understanding the overall message of this part of the word of God?

Because many claim that all the promises made to Israel were conditional. They claim that since Israel failed to keep the conditions, they lost the promises. But Romans 9:10-16 makes it exceedingly plain that God's election is not conditional; that His choices stand, regardless of what men do.

This is stated in great plainness in the 89th Psalm, where God made his eternal promise to David: After the promise was made, God said:

> "If his sons forsake My law
> And do not walk in My judgments,
> If they break My statutes
> And do not keep My commandments,
> Then I will punish their transgression
> with the rod,
> And their iniquity with stripes.

Nevertheless My lovingkindness I will not utterly take from him,

Nor allow My faithfulness to fail.

My covenant I will not break,

Nor alter the word that has gone out of My lips."

(Psalm 89:30-34)

Here God very explicitly said that his promise to David could not even be canceled by sin. He made it clear that He would deal with any sin that might be committed, but that the promise would still stand unchanged. And Romans 9:10-16 teaches us that this is because God's promises to Israel are based upon His election, that is, upon *His* choice, and not upon their obedience.

God's sovereignty in such matters is stressed again in the two verses that follow.

"For the Scripture says to the Pharaoh, *'For this very purpose I have raised you up, that I may show My power in you, and that My name may be declared in all the earth.'* Therefore He has mercy on whom He wills, and whom He wills He hardens." (Romans 9:17-18)

Here God declares that He not only has mercy on whoever He wills, He also hardens whoever He wills.

But this generates a potential problem. Men object to this doctrine because they imagine it would make God unfair. But God's answer is not to explain why this is indeed fair. Instead, He simply says:

> "You will say to me then, 'Why does He still find fault? For who has resisted His will?' But indeed, O man, who are you to reply against God? Will the thing formed say to him who formed *it*, 'Why have you made me like this?' Does not the potter have power over the clay, from the same lump to make one vessel for honor and another for dishonor?" (Romans 9:19-21)

God therefore does not defend this course of action on the basis of its fairness, even though it is fair, but on the basis of His *right*, as the Creator of the entire universe, to do *as He pleases*.

So He continues in Romans 9:22-24:

> *"What* if God, wanting to show *His* wrath and to make His power known, endured with much longsuffering the vessels of wrath prepared for destruction, and that He might make known the riches of His glory on the vessels of mercy, which He had prepared beforehand for glory, *even* us whom He called, not of the Jews only, but also of the Gentiles?"

Again, the point God is making is that He can do *as He pleases*. And He pleases to call not the Jews only, but also the Gentiles. This right of God to do *as He pleases*, and to choose whomsoever He *wants* to choose, is now illustrated by quotations from the Old Testament. The first of these are from Hosea, and are given in Romans 9:25-26.

"As He says also in Hosea: *'I will call them My people, who were not My people, And her beloved, who was not beloved.'* *'And it shall come to pass in the place where it was said to them, '"You are not My people,"' There they shall be called sons of the living God.'"**

The first part of this, *"I will call them My people, who were not My people, And her beloved, who was not beloved."* is a quotation from Hosea 2:23, Where we read,

> **"Then I will sow her for Myself in the earth,**
>
> **And I will have mercy on** *her who had* **not obtained mercy;**
>
> **Then I will say to** *those who were* **not My people,**
>
> **'You** *are* **My people!'**
>
> **And they shall say,**
>
> *'You are* **my God!'"**

The second part, *"And it shall come to pass in the place where it was said to them, 'You are not My people,' There they shall be called sons of the living God."* is a quotation from Hosea 1:10, where we read,

> "Yet the number of the children of Israel
> Shall be as the sand of the sea,
> Which cannot be measured or numbered.
> And it shall come to pass In the place where
> it was said to them,
> 'You *are* not My people,'
> *There* it shall be said to them,
> '*You are* sons of the living God.'"

In both of these quotations, some might imagine that they refer to the church. But a close examination shows that this is cannot even possibly be their meaning. Looking at the last passage first, for it was first in the Order God gave them in Hosea, verses 1-9 of Hosea 1 detail God's rejection of **"the house of Israel."** (verse 8) Then we read the wonderful promise that, even though they were rejected,

> "it shall come to pass
> In the place where it was said to them,
> 'You *are* not My people,'
> *There* it shall be said to them,
> '*You are* sons of the living God.'"

This blessing, **"*You are* sons of the living God,"** was not to be said to someone else, but **"it shall be said to them."** The very ones to whom God had said, **"Lo-ruhamah"** (not pitied) and **"Lo-ammi"** (not my people,) would be told, **"*You are* sons of the living God."** But they would not only be told this, but they would be told this in the very place where they had been so cursed. This conclusion is in the first verse of chapter 2. (We must remember that the chapter and verse divisions in our Bibles were added by man, there were no such divisions in the scriptures when God first gave them. And in some places the divisions actually break up what God was saying.) So God concluded this portion of his holy word by saying, **"Say to your brethren, 'My people,' And to**

your sisters, 'Mercy *is shown*.'" (Hosea 2:1) To whom were these words to be said? To the church? No. They were to be said **"to your brethren."** and **"to your sisters."** Whose **"brethren"** and **"sisters"** were to be told **"My people,"** and **"Mercy *is shown*."**? The very ones to whom it was said **"Lo-ruhamah"** and **"Lo-ammi."** These were unquestionably the sinning **"house of Israel."** No scripture anywhere even suggests the idea that either the church or its individual members are the **"brethren"** and **"sisters"** of the **"house of Israel."**

We find the same thing again in the next portion of Hosea, where God first pronounces his divorce and judgment of guilty Israel; (Hosea 2:2-13) but then, just as in the first chapter, He continues by promising their eventual restoration. (Hosea 2:14-23) Even as He had just pronounced his divorce and judgment, He now promises his betrothal and blessing of the children of that same guilty nation which He had divorced. For even as He had said in verse 2,

> **"Bring charges against your mother, bring charges;**
>
> **For she *is* not My wife, nor *am* I her Husband,"**

He now repeatedly tells them, **"I will betroth you to Me,"** (verses 19 and 20) and says **"you will call Me 'My Husband.'"** (verse 16) God had called the one He had divorced, **"your mother,"** but He now calls the ones He will marry, **"you."** This, then, is the context of verse 23, where we read,

> **"Then I will sow her for Myself in the earth,**
>
> **And I will have mercy on *her who had***
>
> **not obtained mercy;**
>
> **Then I will say to *those who were* not My people,**
>
> **'You *are* My people!'**
>
> **And they shall say,**
>
> **'*You are* my God!'"**

We need to specifically notice that in this scripture, the ones upon whom **"I will have mercy"** are the very same ones **"*who had* not obtained mercy."** And this is unquestionably that guilty ancient nation upon whom God's judgment was about to fall when these words were spoken.

We have taken this detailed look at Hosea 1 and 2 to clearly understand that the two passages from Hosea which the Holy Spirit quoted in Romans 9:25-26 are most certainly not about replacing the physical nation of Israel with a different people, but about a future restoration of that same guilty nation which had previously been rejected for her sin.

But the Holy Spirit, speaking through the Apostle Paul was not finished. He continued by quoting two passages from Isaiah, saying:

"Isaiah also cries out concerning Israel: *'Though the number of the children of Israel be as the sand of the sea, The remnant will be saved. For He will finish the work and cut it short in righteousness, Because the Lord will make a short work upon the earth.'* **And as Isaiah said before:** *'Unless the Lord of Sabaoth had left us a seed, We would have become like Sodom, And we would have been made like Gomorrah.'"* (Romans 9:27-29)

The first of these passages is quoted from Isaiah 10:22-23, Where we read, in the translation which we are using, the NKJV,

> "For though your people,
>
> Israel, be as the sand of the sea,
>
> A remnant of them will return;
>
> The destruction decreed shall overflow with righteousness.
>
> For the Lord GOD of hosts
>
> Will make a determined end In the midst of all the land."

(The difference in wording of the last portion of this passage apparently comes from the process of translating the Old Testament from Hebrew into English and the New Testament passage from Hebrew into Greek and then into English.)

To truly understand the meaning of this short passage from Isaiah, we need to examine it in its context. This is part of a rather long section that runs from verses 5 through 34 of Isaiah 10. This section begins,

> "Woe to Assyria, the rod of My anger
> And the staff in whose hand is My indignation.
> I will send him against an ungodly nation,
> And against the people of My wrath I will give him charge,
> To seize the spoil, to take the prey,
> And to tread them down like the mire of the streets."
>
> (Isaiah 10:5-6)

Most modern Bible scholars have entirely missed the significance of Isaiah 10:5-34 because they have simply (but wrongly) assumed it was only speaking of the attack by the ancient Assyrian king Sennacherib. Thinking it was only speaking of past events, they have neglected this most instructive portion of the word of God. But if they had paid careful attention to this opening passage, they would have realized their error. For Sennacherib attacked Judah during the righteous reign of king Hezekiah, who **"trusted in the LORD God of Israel, so that after him was none like him among all the kings of Judah, nor who were before him. For he held fast to the LORD; he did not depart from following Him, but kept His commandments, which the LORD had commanded Moses."** (2 Kings 18:5-6) And **"Also the hand of God was on Judah to give them singleness of heart to obey the command of the king and the leaders, at the word of the LORD."** (2 Chronicles 30:12)

And **"after these deeds of faithfulness, Sennacherib king of Assyria came and entered Judah; he encamped against the fortified cities, thinking to win them over to himself."** (2 Chronicles 32:1) Hezekiah cried out to the Lord, who answered him, **"I will defend this city, to save it For My own sake and for My servant David's sake."** (Isaiah 37:35)

But in Isaiah 10:6, the Lord says of the king of Assyria that:

> "I will send him against an ungodly nation,
> And against the people of My wrath I will give him charge,
> To seize the spoil, to take the prey,
> And to tread them down like the mire of the streets."

Both Hezekiah and his people had been righteous and the Lord promised to save them from Sennacherib. But in the day described in Isaiah 10 the nation will have been ungodly and He will send Assyria to punish them. Sennacherib was an enemy of God, while this **"Assyrian"** will actually be His agent. Sennacherib indeed attacked in ancient times, but the attack described in this prophecy has never happened, even to this day.

This is highlighted in Isaiah 14, where, immediately after saying the Assyrian (Sennacherib) would be destroyed, (verses 24-27) the Lord added,

> "do not rejoice, all you of Philistia,
> Because the rod that struck you is broken;
> For out of the serpent's roots will come forth
> a viper,
> And its offspring *will be* a fiery flying serpent...
> Wail, O gate! Cry, O city!
> All you of Philistia *are* dissolved;
> For smoke will come from the north,
> And no one *will be* alone in his appointed times." (verses 29-31)

In stating that **"out of the serpent's roots will come forth a viper"** and that **"its offspring *will be* a fiery flying serpent,"** this passage clearly sets forth two separate attacks, one in the past (relative to the time referred to) and one in the future. These two attacks are separated in time by an unspecified number of generations, as the second attacker is the **"offspring"** of the first.

We see this future Assyrian attack again in Micah 5:5-6, where we read that

> "When the Assyrian comes into our land,
> And when he treads in our palaces,
> Then we will raise against him
> Seven shepherds and eight princely men.
> They shall waste with the sword
> the land of Assyria,
> And the land of Nimrod at its entrances;
> Thus He shall deliver *us* from the Assyrian,
> When he comes into our land
> And when he treads within our borders."

This prophecy, which was given at about the same time as that of Isaiah, was never fulfilled in ancient times. When Sennacherib invaded Judea, no one rose to oppose him, much less **"Seven shepherds and eight princely men."** And Israel has never wasted **"the land of Assyria"** **"with the sword."**

But although Isaiah 10:5-6 says this future Assyrian will be God's agent, the next verse says,

> "Yet he does not mean so,
> Nor does his heart think so;
> But *it is* in his heart to destroy,
> And cut off not a few nations."

What is the result?

> "Therefore it shall come to pass, when the Lord has performed all His work on Mount Zion and on Jerusalem, that *He will*

say, "I will punish the fruit of the arrogant heart of the king of Assyria, and the glory of his haughty looks." (Isaiah 10:12)

The reason for this rather long digression has been to help us understand Isaiah 10:20-23, where we read

"And it shall come to pass in that day

That the remnant of Israel,

And such as have escaped of the house of Jacob,

Will never again depend on him who

defeated them,

But will depend on the Lord, the Holy One of Israel, in truth.

The remnant will return, the remnant of Jacob,

To the Mighty God.

For though your people,

O Israel, be as the sand of the sea,

A remnant of them will return;

The destruction decreed shall overflow

with righteousness.

For the Lord GOD of hosts

Will make a determined end

In the midst of all the land.

"Therefore thus says the Lord GOD of hosts: 'O My people, who dwell in Zion, do not be afraid of the Assyrian. He shall strike you with a rod and lift up his staff against you, in the manner of Egypt. For yet a very little while and the indignation will cease, as will My anger in their destruction.' And the Lord of hosts will stir up a scourge for him like the slaughter of Midian at the rock of Oreb; as His rod was on the sea, so will He lift it up in the manner of Egypt. It shall come to pass in that day *That* his burden will be taken away from your

shoulder, And his yoke from your neck, And the yoke will be destroyed because of the anointing oil." (Isaiah 10:24-27)

Thus we clearly see that the context of Isaiah 10:22-23, which is italicized for stress in the quotation above, (it was not italicized in the original) and which the Holy Ghost quoted in Romans 9:27-28, was God's promise of the deliverance of a remnant of Israel during a future attack by an oppressor that the scriptures call **"the Assyrian."**

All this just gives character and meaning to the next quotation the Holy Spirit gave us in this ninth chapter of Romans, **"And as Isaiah said before: 'Unless the Lord of Sabaoth had left us a seed, We would have become like Sodom, And we would have been made like Gomorrah.'"** (Romans 9:29) This is quoted from Isaiah 1:9, where we read:

> **"Unless the Lord of hosts**
>
> **Had left to us a very small remnant,**
>
> **We would have become like Sodom,**
>
> **We would have been made like Gomorrah."**

This is the final sentence in a description of the judgments of God on the guilty nation of Israel. (Isaiah 1:5-9) It is critical to realize what this is really saying. The Holy Spirit is stressing that Israel will *not* be totally destroyed, as were Sodom and Gomorrah. Instead, He would leave a very small remnant of them.

All this discussion of Old Testament scriptures may seem like a distraction, but it is not. Its point has been to make it crystal clear that every one of the Old Testament quotations in Romans 9 has been from a passage that explicitly speaks of the preservation and eventual blessing of a remnant of the ancient nation of Israel. They do not speak of a different people being called Israel in a future day, but of the eventual blessing of the physical descendants of the very people that had been previously rejected for their sins.

At this point the Holy Spirit turns from the future blessing of Israel, and takes up their current status. This is a reversal of what was typically done in the Old Testament prophecies. For they usually first gave Israel's condemnation for its sins, finishing with a promise of eventual restoration. But here the Holy Spirit stresses their eventual restoration before he takes up their present condition. Why this reversal? Because, as we progress through Romans 9-11, we will see that the Holy Spirit, knowing all things and thus knowing what men would say before they said it, answered ahead of time the false doctrine that He has permanently rejected Israel. This is similar to what He did earlier when He said,

> "You will say to me then, 'Why does He still find fault? For who has resisted His will?' But indeed, O man, who are you to reply against God?" (Romans 9:19-20)

But now the Holy Spirit takes up their present status, saying,

> "What shall we say then? That Gentiles, who did not pursue righteousness, have attained to righteousness, even the righteousness of faith; but Israel, pursuing the law of righteousness, has not attained to the law of righteousness. Why? Because *they did* not seek *it* by faith, but as it were, by the works of the law." (Romans 9:30-32a)

So we see that Gentiles had attained righteousness without even pursuing it, because of their faith. But Israel, even though the had pursued righteousness, had not attained to it. The reason is very simple. They had sought righteousness by the works of the law. And **"by the works of the law no flesh shall be justified."** (Galatians 2:16) **"For they stumbled at that stumbling stone. As it is written: 'Behold, I lay in Zion a stumbling stone and rock of offense, And whoever believes on Him will not be put to shame.'"** (Romans 9:32b-33)

As was done before, this is a combination of quotations from two different Old Testament passages. The first of these is:

> "He will be as a sanctuary,
> But a stone of stumbling and a rock of offense
> To both the houses of Israel,
> As a trap and a snare to the inhabitants of Jerusalem." (Isaiah 8:14)

This is typical of God's ways in many places. Since this guilty nation did not want to repent, He gave them a stumbling stone. He came to them in a way that could *only* be received by faith, and those who had no real faith *could not* accept him, even though **"whoever believes in him will not be put to shame."**

The change of subjects is now complete. Since the Holy Spirit is now speaking of Israel's current status, all is on an individual basis. For at the present time Israelites can *only* be blessed as individuals. We see this in the words **"whoever believes in him will not be put to shame."** This is quoted from Isaiah 28:16, where we read,

> "Therefore thus says the Lord GOD:
> 'Behold, I lay in Zion a stone for a foundation,
> A tried stone, a precious cornerstone,
> a sure foundation;
> Whoever believes will not act hastily.'"

Again, the difference in wording, from **"act hastily"** to **"put to shame,"** comes from the difference between translating from the Hebrew directly into English and translating the Hebrew first into Greek and then into English.

The subject now being Israel's current status, the Apostle continues,

> "Brethren, my heart's desire and prayer to God for Israel is that they may be saved. For I bear them witness that they have a zeal for God, but not according to knowledge. For they being ignorant of God's righteousness, and seek-

ing to establish their own righteousness, have not submitted to the righteousness of God. For Christ is the end of the law for righteousness to everyone who believes." (Romans 10:1-4)

Paul never gave up his earnest desire to see all Israel saved. He wanted this so badly that he wrote, as we have already seen, **"I could wish that myself were accursed from Christ for my brethren, my kinsmen according to the flesh."** (Romans 9:3) How many of us have this kind of love for those around us, enough love that we would even be willing, if it were possible, to give up our own salvation if it could save them. But that could never be possible. God has already given the greatest possible sacrifice. If they do not accept that, they cannot be saved. But though Paul loved them so much, he had to point out why they could not be saved. Although they truly have **"a zeal for God,"** that zeal is **"not according to knowledge."** For they are **"seeking to establish their own righteousness"** instead of submitting **"to the righteousness of God."**

How sad and how common is this very basic and almost universal sin. Men are unwilling to admit that in God's sight their own righteousness is really only **"filthy rags,"** as we are told in Isaiah 64:6. Like Cain of old, they want to offer the fruits of their own labors, instead of simply trusting in the blood sacrifice already offered by our Lord Jesus Christ. But **"Christ is the end of the law for righteousness to everyone who believes."** This does not just say that **"Christ is the end of the law,"** But **"Christ is the end of the law for righteousness."** We still value the law, for **"the law was our tutor *to bring us* to Christ, that we might be justified by faith."** (Galatians 3:24) And **"whatever things were written before were written for our learning, that we through the patience and comfort of the Scriptures might have hope."** (Romans 15:4) **"But after faith has come, we are no longer under a tutor."** (Galatians 3:25)

We remember that earlier in this same epistle, the Holy Spirit had already said, **"Do we then make void the law through faith? Certainly not! On the contrary, we establish the law."** (Romans 3:31) The law has indeed passed away, but only for those who in faith have trusted in the blood of the Lord Jesus Christ as atonement for their sins. For any who seek justification through the law, it is still in force, for the Holy Spirit warns all of these that they are debtors **"to keep the whole law."** (Galatians 5:3) And He warns them that **"whoever shall keep the whole law, and yet stumble in one *point*, he is guilty of all."** (James 2:10) Since we are all sinners, when we put ourselves under the law, it can only curse us, as we read,

> **"For as many as are of the works of the law are under the curse; for it is written, 'Cursed is everyone who does not continue in all things which are written in the book of the law, to do them.' But that no one is justified by the law in the sight of God *is* evident, for 'the just shall live by faith.' Yet the law is not of faith, but 'the man who does them shall live by them.'"** (Galatians 3:10-12)

There are very few that would pretend they are perfect. Yet the law blesses only the perfect. It curses anyone who is not perfect. But **"Christ has redeemed us from the curse of the law, having become a curse for us (for it is written, 'Cursed is everyone who hangs on a tree.')"** (Galatians 3:13)

Returning now to Romans 10, the Holy Spirit reminds us, **"For Moses writes about the righteousness which is of the law, 'The man who does those things shall live by them.'"** (Romans 10:5) This is a quotation from Leviticus 18:5, where we read, **"You shall therefore keep My statutes and My judgments, which if a man does, he shall live by them: I *am* the Lord."**

We need to realize that this promise is not a promise of eternal salvation. It is only a promise of life in this earth. The fact that every one of them died is proof that not even one of them ever kept the law.

The Holy Spirit then continues,

> **"But the righteousness of faith speaks in this way, 'Do not say in your heart, "Who will ascend into heaven?"' (that is, to bring Christ down from above) or, '"Who will descend into the abyss?"' (that is, to bring Christ up from the dead). But what does it say? 'The word is near you, in your mouth and in your heart' (that is, the word of faith which we preach):"** (Romans 10:6-8)

This series of quotations is from Deuteronomy 30, where we read,

> "For this commandment which I command you today *is* not *too* mysterious for you, nor is it far off. It is not in heaven, that you should say, 'Who will ascend into heaven for us and bring it to us, that we may hear it and do it?' Nor is it beyond the sea, that you should say, 'Who will go over the sea for us and bring it to us, that we may hear it and do it?' But the word is very near you, in your mouth and in your heart, that you may do it." (Deuteronomy 30:11-14)

The point here is that we should just believe the message of the gospel, **"the word of faith which we preach,"** rather than ask how it could possibly be true. For the message is easy to understand.

And what is this **"word of faith which we preach"**? **"That if you confess with your mouth the Lord Jesus and believe in your heart that God has raised Him from the dead, you will be saved."** (Romans 10:9)

This is the pure, simple gospel of Jesus Christ, the way to be saved. **"For with the heart one believes unto righteousness, and with the mouth confession is made unto salvation."** (Romans 10:10) And it is for everyone. Whether someone is Jew or Greek has no bearing on the simple offer of salvation.

"For the Scripture says, *'Whoever believes on Him will not be put to shame.'* For there is no distinction between Jew and Greek, for the same Lord over all is rich to all who call upon Him. For *'whoever calls on the name of the Lord shall be saved.'"* (Romans 10:11-13)

The first of these quotations is from Isaiah 28:16, which says,

> "Therefore thus says the Lord GOD:
> 'Behold, I lay in Zion a stone for a foundation,
> A tried stone, a precious cornerstone,
> a sure foundation;
> Whoever believes will not act hastily.'"

The second one is from Joel 2:32,

> "And it shall come to pass
> That whoever calls on the name of the Lord
> Shall be saved.
> For in Mount Zion and in Jerusalem
> there shall be deliverance,
> As the Lord has said,
> Among the remnant whom the Lord calls."

The Holy Spirit quotes these to show that this is not a new doctrine. It had been revealed in the Old Testament, the scriptures they already had. But here He explicitly points out that these scriptures, which had been given long before, clearly showed that this **"word of faith"** would go out to all nations, not just to the Jews.

Many have made a bad usage of this principle to deny that there is still a future program for Israel. But this says no such thing. It only says that the same **"word of faith"** is offered to all, Jew or Greek. There is no suggestion whatsoever that Israel is fused into the church. This idea is not taught here or anywhere else in the entire word of God. If the Bible indeed taught such an idea, that would directly contradict the central message of Romans 9-11, as well as many Old Testament scriptures.

But now the Holy Spirit continues,

> **"How then shall they call on Him in whom they have not believed? And how shall they believe in Him of whom they have not heard? And how shall they hear without a preacher? And how shall they preach unless they are sent? As it is written: 'How beautiful are the feet of those who preach the gospel of peace, Who bring glad tidings of good things!'"** (Romans 10:14-15)

The quotation here actually comes from two Old Testament scriptures. It is not a combination of two Old Testament scriptures, as some of the others have been, but a statement that occurs twice in the Old Testament. The first of these is

> "**How beautiful upon the mountains**
> **Are the feet of him who brings good news,**
> **Who proclaims peace,**
> **Who brings glad tidings of good** *things*,
> **Who proclaims salvation,**
> **Who says to Zion,**
> **'Your God reigns!'"** (Isaiah 52:7)

And the second is

> "**Behold, on the mountains**
> **The feet of him who brings good tidings,**
> **Who proclaims peace!"** (Nahum 1:15)

But the Holy Spirit had asked, **"how shall they preach unless they are sent?** Sadly, many preach or teach just because they want to, **"desiring to be teachers of the law, understanding neither what they say nor the things which they affirm."** (1 Timothy 1:7) These self-appointed preachers or teachers often do more harm than good.

> "For of this sort are those who creep into households and make captives of gullible women loaded down with sins, led away by various lusts, always learning and never able to come to the knowledge of the truth. Now as Jannes and Jambres resisted Moses, so do these also resist the truth: men of corrupt minds, disapproved concerning the faith; but they will progress no further, for their folly will be manifest to all, as theirs also was." (2 Timothy 3:6-9)

But here the Holy Spirit's basic subject is the present status of Israel, so He continues,

> **"But they have not all obeyed the gospel. For Isaiah says, *'Lord, who has believed our report?'"*** (Romans 10:16)
>
> This is a quotation from Isaiah's description of Israel's rejection of their Messiah, **"Who has believed our report? And to whom has the arm of the Lord been revealed?"** (Isaiah 53:1)

As the Holy Spirit had already pointed out, these rejecters of their own Messiah did not have faith. So He adds, **"So then faith *comes* by hearing, and hearing by the word of God."** (Romans 10:17) It is only by hearing the truth of the word of God that faith can come. And **"The entirety of Your word *is* truth"** (Psalm 119:160) This concept is critical. We need to consider *all* of the word of God, not just part of it. For **"Every word of God *is* pure,"** (Proverbs 30:5) and Jesus himself said **"It is written, *'Man shall not live by bread alone, but by every word of God.'"*** (Luke 4:4) This was a quotation from Deuteronomy 8:3, Where we read,

> **"He humbled you, allowed you to hunger, and fed you with manna which you did not know nor did your fathers know, that He might make you know that man shall not live by bread alone; but man lives by every *word* that proceeds from the mouth of the Lord."**

Those who choose to ignore anything the word of God says are willfully blinding themselves. And anyone who listens to such a false "teacher" will be led astray.

The Holy Spirit continues his message, saying, **"But I say, have they not heard? Yes indeed: *'Their sound has gone out to all the earth, And their words to the ends of the world.'"*** (Romans 10:18) Some imagine that this is some kind of a call to Israel to be a missionary witnesses to the entire world. But when we examine the quotation in this verse, we see otherwise. That quotation, in its original context, is:

> "The heavens declare the glory of God;
> And the firmament shows His handiwork.
> Day unto day utters speech,
> And night unto night reveals knowledge.
> *There is* no speech nor language
> *Where* their voice is not heard.
> Their line has gone out through all the earth,
> And their words to the end of the world." (Psalm 19:1-4)

So we see that the sound referred to is the testimony of creation, not the words of any man, whether Jew or Gentile.

And now the Holy Spirit asks? **"But I say, did Israel not know?"** (Romans 10:19a) This question is addressed towards the point He has been making, that the **"word of faith"** has now **"gone out to all the earth."** So He now demonstrates that it had been plainly stated in the Old Testament scriptures, the ones Israel already had, even before Jesus came. So He gives two examples, and a scriptural statement of the reason for this action.

The first example is, **"First Moses says: 'I will provoke you to jealousy by those who are not a nation, I will move you to anger by a foolish nation.'"** (Romans 10:19b) This is a quotation from Deuteronomy 32:21, where we read, **"They have provoked Me to jealousy by *what* is not God; They have moved Me to anger by their foolish idols. But I will provoke them to jealousy by *those who are* not a nation; I will move them to anger by a foolish nation."** Here we are told that God, in his jealousy over their unfaithfulness to himself will take action to provoke them to jealousy.

In considering this, we need to realize what jealousy is in a love relationship. In this context jealousy is the feeling a person experiences when someone they love gives their love to someone else, instead of to themselves. So God was jealous because they worshiped false gods. And He said He would provoke them to jealousy by giving his love to others. We need to particularly notice what God is saying here. Some imagine that this means that God's rejection of Israel is final and permanent.

But an act designed to provoke jealousy is the very opposite of a final rejection. It is an act designed to win back a lost love. So this act of God was not a permanent rejection of Israel, but an effort to win back its love. And other scriptures tell us that this will eventually happen. For in a coming day

> "*he who is* **left in Zion and remains in Jerusalem will be called holy—everyone who is recorded among the living in Jerusalem.**" (Isaiah 4:3)

and

> "**No more shall every man teach his neighbor, and every man his brother, saying, 'Know the Lord,' for they all shall know Me, from the least of them to the greatest of them.**" (Jeremiah 31:34)

And in considering this scripture, it is important to notice who the Holy Spirit was speaking of, when He said that **"they all shall know Me, from the least of them to the greatest of them."** Three verses earlier these had been clearly defined as **"the house of Israel"** and **"the house of Judah"** (Jeremiah 31:31) Now, although it is misinterpretation, there is some excuse in the scriptures to imagine that **"the house of Israel"** actually means "the church." But there is no scripture anywhere that contains even the slightest pretension of an excuse to even imagine that the term **"the house of Judah"** actually means "the church." So this promise was unquestionably made to the physical nation of Israel, not to the church. And what was the promise? That a day was coming when

> "**No more shall every man teach his neighbor, and every man his brother, saying, 'Know the Lord,' for they all shall know Me, from the least of them to the greatest of them.**" (Jeremiah 31:34)

The second of the two examples the Holy Spirit gave here is:

> "**But Isaiah is very bold and says:** *'I was found by those who did not seek Me; I was made manifest to those who did not ask for Me.'*" (Romans 10:20)

This is a quotation from Isaiah 65:1, which says,

> "**I was sought by** *those who* **did not ask** *for Me*;
> **I was found by** *those who* **did not seek Me.**
> **I said, 'Here I am, here I am,'**
> **To a nation** *that* **was not called by My name."**

Again, we see that this had been foretold long before it happened. But why did God do this?

His stated reason for it is very interesting, for God had originally given it as the reason He said He would be **"found by** *those who* **did not seek"** him. The reason the Holy Spirit gave for this is, **"But to Israel he says: 'All day long I have stretched out My hands To a disobedient and contrary people.'"** (Romans 10:21) We remember that the second example we just examined was from Isaiah 65:1. The reason given by the Holy Spirit had been given in the very next sentence, the first sentence of Isaiah 65:2. **"I have stretched out My hands all day long to a rebellious people."** So we see that God turned aside to the Gentiles because, and specifically because, Israel had rebelled. But while this is true, we must remember that His turning aside to the Gentiles was not an act of final rejection. It was an act designed to provoke them to jealousy, that is, to win their hearts back to Himself.

This is not just an interpretation of scripture. It is explicitly stated in the beginning of the next chapter. We must remember that the chapter and verse divisions were added by man. This was simply the next few sentences of the epistle to the Romans as it was originally written. So we read:

> "**I say then, has God cast away His people? Certainly not! For I also am an Israelite, of the seed of Abraham,** *of* **the tribe of Benjamin. God has not cast away His people whom He foreknew."** (Romans 11:1-2a)

How could the Holy Spirit, in speaking through the Apostle Paul, have made this more clear? **"God has not cast away his people."** This is stated in so many ways that it is mind boggling.

He continues,

> **"Or do you not know what the Scripture says of Elijah, how he pleads with God against Israel, saying, 'Lord, they have killed Your prophets and torn down Your altars, and I alone am left, and they seek my life'? But what does the divine response say to him? 'I have reserved for Myself seven thousand men who have not bowed the knee to Baal.' Even so then, at this present time there is a remnant according to the election of grace."** (Romans 11:2b-5)

Elijah's accusation had been made twice. The first time was:

> "So he said, 'I have been very zealous for the Lord God of hosts; for the children of Israel have forsaken Your covenant, torn down Your altars, and killed Your prophets with the sword. I alone am left; and they seek to take my life.'" (1 Kings 19:10)

Then, in another place, we read again:

> "And he said, 'I have been very zealous for the Lord God of hosts; because the children of Israel have forsaken Your covenant, torn down Your altars, and killed Your prophets with the sword. I alone am left; and they seek to take my life.'" (1 Kings 19:14)

But God had answered him,

> "Yet I have reserved seven thousand in Israel, all whose knees have not bowed to Baal, and every mouth that has not kissed him." (1 Kings 19:18)

The Holy Spirit gave this example of one of the worst periods in Israel's sad history to show that He has always preserved a remnant of his people, even as He does to this day. And that remnant is **"according to the election of grace."**

So the Holy Spirit goes on,

> **"And if by grace, then *it is* no longer of works; otherwise grace is no longer grace. But if *it is* of works, it is no longer grace; otherwise work is no longer work."** (Romans 11:6)

Thus the Holy Spirit ties together what He has been saying, in two short sentences pointing out that He reserves to himself the right to choose who will receive his mercy, and also pointing out that his mercy comes entirely by his grace, and works have nothing to do with it.

He then continues,

> **"What then? Israel has not obtained what it seeks; but the elect have obtained it, and the rest were blinded. Just as it is written: 'God has given them a spirit of stupor, Eyes that they should not see And ears that they should not hear, To this very day.'"** (Romans 11:7-8)

As He had so often done before, the Holy Spirit here quoted two Old Testament scriptures together. The first one was,

> **"Yet the Lord has not given you a heart to perceive and eyes to see and ears to hear, to this *very* day."** (Deuteronomy 29:4)

And the second was,

> **"For the Lord has poured out on you**
> **The spirit of deep sleep,**
> **And has closed your eyes, namely, the prophets;**
> **And He has covered your heads, *namely*, the seers."**
>
> (Isaiah 29:10)

It was the leaders of Israel that had caused the people to turn aside from the pure word of God. But since the blindness was willful, both on the part of the leaders and on the part of the people, God responded with a judicial blindness, making repentance *impossible*. He had said this before, in the time of Isaiah, and He said it again when Jesus was here, for we read that

> "**Therefore they could not believe, because Isaiah said again:** *'He has blinded their eyes and hardened their hearts, Lest they should see with their eyes, Lest they should understand with their hearts and turn, So that I should heal them.'*" (John 12:39-40)

This was quoted from Isaiah 6:10, where we read,

> "Make the heart of this people dull,
>
> And their ears heavy,
>
> And shut their eyes;
>
> Lest they see with their eyes,
>
> And hear with their ears,
>
> And understand with their heart,
>
> And return and be healed."

We also find this same principle in action in Romans 1:24-25, where we read,

> "**Therefore God also gave them up to uncleanness, in the lusts of their hearts, to dishonor their bodies among themselves, who exchanged the truth of God for the lie, and worshiped and served the creature rather than the Creator, who is blessed forever. Amen.**"

The Holy Spirit stated this again in his very next quotation from the Old Testament.

> "And David says: *'Let their table become a snare and a trap, A stumbling block and a recompense to them. Let their eyes be darkened, so that they do not see, And bow down their back always.'*" (Romans 11:9-10)

This was a quotation from Psalm 69:22-23, which says,

> "Let their table become a snare before them,
> And their well-being a trap.
> Let their eyes be darkened, so that they do not see;
> And make their loins shake continually."

So we see that our God was stressing that He had inflicted a judicial blindness upon those that had rejected His message through His only begotten Son. Because of their hardened rebellion against Himself, He had *intentionally* put a stumbling block in their way. But He is not finished with them yet, as we shall see in the next few verses.

For the Holy Spirit continues,

> "I say then, have they stumbled that they should fall? Certainly not! But through their fall, to provoke them to jealousy, salvation *has come* to the Gentiles. Now if their fall *is* riches for the world, and their failure riches for the Gentiles, how much more their fullness! For I speak to you Gentiles; inasmuch as I am an apostle to the Gentiles, I magnify my ministry, if by any means I may provoke to jealousy *those who are* my flesh and save some of them. For if their being cast away is the reconciling of the world, what *will* their acceptance *be* but life from the dead?" (Romans 11:11-15)

How much more clearly could the Holy Spirit have stated this? They were not caused to stumble **"that they should fall,"** but to provoke them to jealousy. We have already noticed that this act of provoking to jealousy is an act designed to restore a relationship, not an act of final rejection. So the Apostle Paul was earnest in his ministry in hopes of provoking jealousy in **"*those who are* my flesh,"** in hopes of saving **"some of them." But these statements are interspersed with two others of even greater significance. These are, **"Now if their fall *is* riches for the world, and their failure riches for the Gentiles, how much more their fullness!"** and **"For if their being cast away is the reconciling of the world, what *will* their acceptance *be* but life from the dead?"** These last two statements highlight two things. First, they both refer to Israel's future acceptance, and second, they answer the unbelieving complaint that preferring Israel in a future day would be unjust. God here is stressing that when Israel is finally once again accepted, it will be such blessing for the Gentiles as to seem as if they had risen from the dead.

The Holy Spirit now begins a solemn warning to those that He knew would in a future day deny this wonderful truth.

> "For if the firstfruit *is* holy, the lump *is* also *holy*; and if the root *is* holy, so *are* the branches. And if some of the branches were broken off, and you, being a wild olive tree, were grafted in among them, and with them became a partaker of the root and fatness of the olive tree, do not boast against the branches. But if you do boast, *remember that* you do not support the root, but the root supports you. You will say then, 'Branches were broken off that I might be grafted in.' Well *said*. Because of unbelief they were broken off, and you stand by faith. Do not be haughty, but fear. For if God did not spare the natural branches, He may not spare you either. Therefore consider the goodness and severity of God: on those who fell, severity; but toward you, goodness, if you continue in *His* goodness. Otherwise you also will be cut off." (Romans 11:16-22)

This is not just an idle threat. When we study the history of the church, we find that at about the same time as the almost universal acceptance of the doctrine that Israel was permanently set aside, the "church" also lost the central essence of doctrine of salvation, that it is **"by grace... through faith"** and is **"the gift of God, not of works."** (Ephesians 2:8-9) This was the beginning of what we call "the dark ages," a period of well over thousand years in which "the church" taught salvation by works, not by faith. Indeed, they were cut off the tree of blessing, even as these ancient Jews had been. For it is **"not by works of righteousness which we have done, but according to His mercy He saved us."** (Titus 3:5)

But after this warning, the Holy Spirit continues with his subject, saying,

> "And they also, if they do not continue in unbelief, will be grafted in, for God is able to graft them in again. For if you were cut out of the olive tree which is wild by nature, and were grafted contrary to nature into a cultivated olive tree, how much more will these, who *are* natural *branches*, be grafted into their own olive tree?" (Romans 11:23-25)

Here God stresses his ability to graft these, the natural branches, back into their own olive tree. Many have stressed the application of this principle to individual Jews in the present day. And that application is both true and appropriate, for today God will graft any believing Jew back into that olive tree of blessing. But that is not the only correct application of this promise.

The promise has a condition attached to it. That condition is **"if they do not continue in unbelief."** God has explicitly promised that if Israel does **"not continue in unbelief,"** He will graft them back into their own olive tree. This promise is indeed conditional, and thus will not be kept unless Israel indeed does **"not continue in unbelief."** But if that is the case, how can God have so explicitly promised their eventual restoration in so many places? It is because He, who declares **"the end from the beginning"** (Isaiah 46:10) Has already told us, in no uncertain language, that in a future day they will indeed **"not continue in unbelief."** We have already noticed two scriptures about this, that in a coming day,

> *"he who is* left in Zion and remains in Jerusalem will be called holy—everyone who is recorded among the living in Jerusalem." (Isaiah 4:3)

and

> "No more shall every man teach his neighbor, and every man his brother, saying, 'Know the Lord,' for they all shall know Me, from the least of them to the greatest of them." (Jeremiah 31:34)

But now we need to notice several others.

The repentance that will bring about this state is explicitly described in Zechariah 12:10-14, saying:

> "I will pour on the house of David and on the inhabitants of Jerusalem the Spirit of grace and supplication; then they will look on Me whom they pierced. Yes, they will mourn for Him as one mourns for *his* only *son*, and grieve for Him as one grieves for a firstborn. In that day there shall be a great mourning in Jerusalem, like the mourning at Hadad Rimmon in the plain of Megiddo. And the land shall mourn, every family by itself: the family of the house of David by itself, and their wives by themselves; the family of the house of Nathan by itself, and their wives by themselves; the family of the house of Levi by itself, and their wives by themselves; the family of Shimei by itself, and their wives by themselves; all the families that remain, every family by itself, and their wives by themselves."

We have already noticed Isaiah 1:9, where we read,

> "Unless the Lord of hosts
> Had left to us a very small remnant,
> We would have become like Sodom,
> We would have been made like Gomorrah."

Those who repent in the way we have just seen will indeed be only a very small remnant, for this will only take place after

> "'it shall come to pass in all the land,'
> Says the Lord,
> '*That* two-thirds in it shall be cut off and die,
> But *one*-third shall be left in it:
> I will bring the *one*-third through the fire,

> Will refine them as silver is refined,
>
> And test them as gold is tested.'"
>
> (Zechariah 13:8-9a)

Some have quite incorrectly imagined that this speaks of the time of the time of Titus, when he was used by God to destroy guilty Judea. But there is no way to even pretend that at that time two-thirds of all those in the land died, and all the rest became believers as described in the rest of this passage in the words,

> "They will call on My name,
>
> And I will answer them.
>
> I will say, 'This *is* My people';
>
> And each one will say, 'The Lord is my God.'" (Zechariah 13:9b)

The prophesied repentance will also be after the time of which we read that:

> "'As I live,' says the Lord GOD, 'surely with a mighty hand, with an outstretched arm, and with fury poured out, I will rule over you. I will bring you out from the peoples and gather you out of the countries where you are scattered, with a mighty hand, with an outstretched arm, and with fury poured out. And I will bring you into the wilderness of the peoples, and there I will plead My case with you face to face. Just as I pleaded My case with your fathers in the wilderness of the land of Egypt, so I will plead My case with you,' says the Lord GOD. 'I will make you pass under the rod, and I will bring you into the bond of the covenant; I will purge the rebels from among you, and those who transgress against Me; I will bring them out of the country where they dwell, but they shall not enter the land of Israel. Then you will know that I *am* the Lord.'" (Ezekiel 20:33-38)

So the God who cannot lie has told us that He will bring Judah through a time of intense trouble that will kill a full two-thirds of them, and after that He will personally purge out all the rebels from the midst of the returning Israelites. Then, after that time, all of them that are left will truly repent and turn to him with their whole hearts. Anyone who denies that this will indeed happen is denying explicitly stated scripture.

But before leaving the subject, the Holy Spirit once again stressed this eventual restoration of Israel, saying,

> **"For I do not desire, brethren, that you should be ignorant of this mystery, lest you should be wise in your own opinion, that blindness in part has happened to Israel until the fullness of the Gentiles has come in. And so all Israel will be saved, as it is written:** *'The Deliverer will come out of Zion, And He will turn away ungodliness from Jacob; For this is My covenant with them, When I take away their sins.'"* (Romans 11:25-27)

The quotation here is from Isaiah 59:20-21, where we read:

> "'The Redeemer will come to Zion, And to those who turn from transgression in Jacob,' Says the Lord. 'As for Me,' says the Lord, 'this *is* My covenant with them: My Spirit who *is* upon you, and My words which I have put in your mouth, shall not depart from your mouth, nor from the mouth of your descendants, nor from the mouth of your descendants' descendants," says the Lord, "from this time and forevermore."'

So once again, we see that the Old Testament passage quoted by the Holy Spirit was another one about the future restoration of Israel. How do we know it is not speaking of the present age? Someone who trusts in the Lord Jesus today receives salvation. But that salvation is not promised to their **"descendants"** and to their **"descendant's descendants... from this time and forevermore."**

This is common language for promises to Israel, but no similar promise was ever made to the church, not even once. Furthermore, the people to whom this promise was made were specifically defined as

"those who turn from transgression in Jacob." And as we noted earler, although there is some excuse for mistakenly imagining that when our God says **"Israel,"** he actually means "the church," there is not even the slightest excuse, anywhere inthe entire Bible, for even imagining that the name **"Jacob"** was ever used in speaking of "the church." So, like the previous scripture we examined, this is unquestionaby speaking of a future revival of the ancient nation of Israel, not of "the church."

But returning now to Romans 11, we need to notice that the Holy Spirit defined a distinct limit to the time of Israel's partial blindness. It was to last **"until the fullness of the gentiles has come in."** Some want to pretend that this refers to the time of Jerusalem's destruction in AD 70. But we see differently in the place where Jesus clearly predicted that destruction. For Jesus said,

> **"when you see Jerusalem surrounded by armies, then know that its desolation is near. Then let those who are in Judea flee to the mountains, let those who are in the midst of her depart, and let not those who are in the country enter her. For these are the days of vengeance, that all things which are written may be fulfilled. But woe to those who are pregnant and to those who are nursing babies in those days! For there will be great distress in the land and wrath upon this people. And they will fall by the edge of the sword, and be led away captive into all nations. And Jerusalem will be trampled by Gentiles until the times of the Gentiles are fulfilled."** (Luke 21:20-24)

Here we see clearly described the coming of the Roman armies and the instruction to flee when this happens. Jesus explicitly said it would be **"the days of vengeance, that all things that are written may be fulfilled."** It is obvious that this could not mean that this was when absolutely everything written would be fulfilled, for there are many prophecies about other things. So it clearly means that at that time, all things written about the time Jesus was speaking of would be fulfilled. That indeed came to pass at the hands of the Romans, including, exactly as Jesus said, "great distress in the land and wrath upon this people. And they will fall by the edge of the sword, and be led away captive into all nations."

We know from history, and even from logic if we did not know the history, that they were not **"led away captive into all nations"** until after Jerusalem was destroyed.

But it is only after this that we read, **"And Jerusalem will be trampled by Gentiles until the times of the Gentiles are fulfilled."** So we see, just from the stated order of the events Jesus referred to, that the time of trampling *began* when Jerusalem was destroyed. It did not *end* at that time. It *began* at that time. And it is still going on. For even to this very day, Jerusalem is still being **"trampled by Gentiles."** This clearly demonstrates that **"the times of the Gentiles"** are not yet **"fulfilled."**

Thus we see that **"the fullness of the gentiles"** has even yet not **"come in,"** and thus Israel's time of **"blindness in part"** is not yet ended. But it will end when **"the fullness of the gentiles has come in."** This, then, is the context of the Holy Spirit's statement, **"And so all Israel will be saved."**

This is again demonstrated by what He said next,

> "Concerning the gospel they are enemies for your sake, but concerning the election they are beloved for the sake of the fathers. For the gifts and the calling of God are irrevocable." (Romans 11:28-29)

We first need to notice that the subject here is most definitely not the church. For the ones under discussion are called **"they,"** not "we," and **"Concerning the gospel they are enemies for your sake."** This very clearly shows that the people being spoken of are not Christians, not the church. But then what does the Holy Spirit say about them? **"But concerning the election they are beloved for the sake of the fathers."** So we see that these ones, who are most definitely not the church, **"are beloved for the sake of the fathers."** Thus we are directed back to Abraham, Isaac, And Jacob, the fathers of Israel, to whom the promises were made.

Further, this is **"concerning the election."** Many assume that whenever we find the term **"the elect"** in scripture, it is always speaking of the church. But here the concept is applied to these ones who are **"enemies," "concerning the gospel."** We find that Israel is called **"my elect"** three times in the book of Isaiah. The first of these is,

"For Jacob My servant's sake,

And Israel My elect,

I have even called you by your name;

I have named you, though you have not known Me." (Isaiah 45:4)

The second one is,

"I will bring forth descendants from Jacob,

And from Judah an heir of My mountains;

My elect shall inherit it,

And My servants shall dwell there."

(Isaiah 65:9)

And the third one is,

"I will rejoice in Jerusalem,

And joy in My people;

The voice of weeping shall no longer be heard

in her,

Nor the voice of crying.

No more shall an infant from there *live but*

a few days,

Nor an old man who has not fulfilled his days;

For the child shall die one hundred years old,

But the sinner *being* one hundred years old

> shall be accursed.
> They shall build houses and inhabit *them*;
> They shall plant vineyards and eat their fruit.
> They shall not build and another inhabit;
> They shall not plant and another eat;
> For as the days of a tree, *so shall be*
> the days of My people,
> And My elect shall long enjoy the work
> of their hands." (Isaiah 65:19-22)

Finally, the Holy Spirit gives his basic, essential reason for all this. **"For the gifts and the calling of God are irrevocable."** (Romans 11:29) This is the reason the fleshly descendants of the ancient nation of Israel *must* be restored to their land and blessed there. That reason is the faithfulness of God. It has nothing to do with the faithfulness of Israel, or with the lack thereof. It is based entirely on who God is, and what He is. He made promises to his ancient people, and He will keep those promises. Some imagine that his promises were not absolute, but only conditional. They say that since Israel did not fulfill the conditions, they lost the promises. But as we have already noticed, God has clearly stated otherwise, saying,

> "My mercy I will keep for him forever,
> And My covenant shall stand firm with him.
> His seed also I will make to *endure* forever,
> And his throne as the days of heaven.
> If his sons forsake My law
> And do not walk in My judgments,
> If they break My statutes
> And do not keep My commandments,
> Then I will punish their transgression with the rod,

And their iniquity with stripes.
Nevertheless My lovingkindness I will not utterly take from him,
Nor allow My faithfulness to fail.
My covenant I will not break,
Nor alter the word that has gone out of My lips.
Once I have sworn by My holiness;
I will not lie to David:
His seed shall endure forever,
And his throne as the sun before Me;
It shall be established forever like the moon,
Even *like* the faithful witness in the sky." (Psalm 89:28-37)

We already noticed that in this place God explicitly said that not even sin could cancel his covenant. He said that if they sinned, he would deal with that sin. But

"nevertheless My lovingkindness I will not utterly take from him,
Nor allow My faithfulness to fail."

and then He added,

"My covenant I will not break,
Nor alter the word that has gone out of My lips."

God closed this passage by saying that David's throne would be

> "as the sun before Me;
> It shall be established forever like the moon,
> Even *like* the faithful witness in the sky."

He later expanded on this, saying,

> "Thus says the Lord: 'If you can break My covenant with the day and My covenant with the night, so that there will not be day and night in their season, then My covenant may also be broken with David My servant, so that he shall not have a son to reign on his throne, and with the Levites, the priests, My ministers. As the host of heaven cannot be numbered, nor the sand of the sea measured, so will I multiply the descendants of David My servant and the Levites who minister to Me.'" (Jeremiah 33:20-22)

Some will protest that the promise to David was fulfilled in Jesus. But we need to notice that this promise includes not only **"a son to reign on his throne."** It also includes **"the Levites, the priests, My ministers."** Levites and priests are parts of Jewish worship. They have no place in Christian worship.

Is there any way God could have been more absolute in saying all this? The Holy Spirit has now finished the basic message of these three chapters, but he added a little more at the end, saying,

> **"For as you were once disobedient to God, yet have now obtained mercy through their disobedience, even so these also have now been disobedient, that through the mercy shown you they also may obtain mercy. For God has committed them all to disobedience, that He might have mercy on all."** (Romans 11:30-32)

God has used the disobedience of Israel as occasion to give mercy to all, so that same mercy, being now offered to all, may come back to Israel. For God has found all disobedient, that he might have mercy on all.

This brings forth a wonderful doxology as a conclusion to these three chapters.

> **"Oh, the depth of the riches both of the wisdom and knowledge of God! How unsearchable are His judgments and His ways past finding out!** *'For who has known the mind of the Lord? Or who has become His counselor?' 'Or who has first given to Him And it shall be repaid to him?'* **For of Him and through Him and to Him are all things, to whom be glory forever. Amen."** (Romans 11:33-36)

The first quotation here is from Isaiah 40;13,

> **"Who has directed the Spirit of the Lord,**
> **Or as His counselor has taught Him?"**

And the second one is from Job 41:11, where God said,

> **"Who has preceded Me, that I should pay him? Everything under heaven is Mine."**

Again, the different translation procedures rendered slight differences in the wording.

We have examined this three chapter section in greater detail than the other sections to clearly demonstrate what the Holy Spirit was actually saying here. The current rejection of Israel is only temporarily. In the future, she will again be restored and blessed, because **"the gifts and the calling of God are irrevocable."** (Romans 11:29) this section states this so plainly, so many times, and in so many ways, that nothing but the blindness of unbelieving prejudice can keep anyone from seeing it.

And it is the **"irrevocable"** nature of God's **"gifts"** and **"calling"** that gives strength to the faith which figures so strongly in the first eight chapters of this epistle. So, rather than being a totally different subject, this section reinforces, and not only reinforces, but *strongly* reinforces, the faith presented in the first eight chapters of this epistle.

Section

CHAPTER 12:1 – 15:13

Christian Service

Having presented the normal development of a Christian and the total reliability of God, the Holy Spirit now moves into Christian service. As noted in the introduction, this is really just a practical outworking of the truths presented in the first two sections. So this section opens with a plea based on the word **"therefore."** That is, this plea is based on what had been presented in the previous part of this epistle. And what is that? The basis of our faith, the reliability of God. Since our God is *absolutely* reliable,

> "I beseech you therefore, brethren, by the mercies of God, that you present your bodies a living sacrifice, holy, acceptable to God, *which is* your reasonable service. And do not be conformed to this world, but be transformed by the renewing of your mind, that you may prove what *is* that good and acceptable and perfect will of God." (Romans 12:1-2)

The first part of this plea, to **"present your bodies a living sacrifice, holy, acceptable to God,"** brings to mind that old refrain:

I surrender all.

I surrender all.

All to Jesus I surrender,

I surrender all.

Being **"a living sacrifice"** is **"patient continuance in doing good."**(Romans 2:7) But this is only **"your reasonable service."** Remember our Lord's exhortation that

> **"When you have done all those things which you are commanded, say, 'We are unprofitable servants. We have done what was our duty to do.' "** (Luke 17:10)

If we really give our all for Christ, if we serve Him faithfully for our entire lives. We will have only done what is **"reasonable,"** only what had been **"our duty to do."**

So we are not to be **"conformed to this world,"** but to be **"transformed."** How? **"By the renewing of your mind."** As we are told in another scripture,

> **"Let this mind be in you which was also in Christ Jesus, who, being in the form of God, did not consider it robbery to be equal with God, but made Himself of no reputation, taking the form of a bondservant,** *and* **coming in the likeness of men. And being found in appearance as a man, He humbled Himself and became obedient to** *the point of* **death, even the death of the cross."** (Philippians 2:5-8)

And in this way we will **"prove what is that good and acceptable and perfect will of God."**

Having made this appeal, the Holy Spirit develops this into the main subject of this section of the epistle, which is Christian service. So we read:

> "For I say, through the grace given to me, to everyone who is among you, not to think *of himself* more highly than he ought to think, but to think soberly, as God has dealt to each one a measure of faith. For as we have many members in one body, but all the members do not have the same function, so we, *being* many, are one body in Christ, and individually members of one another." (Romans 12:3-5)

How easy it is for those who have the more flashy gifts to begin to think they are more important than others who have less noticeable gifts. The church indeed could not function without preachers and teachers. But how well could it operate without cooks and janitors? We read in another scripture that

> "... those members of the body which seem to be weaker are necessary. And those *members* of the body which we think to be less honorable, on these we bestow greater honor; and our unpresentable *parts* have greater modesty, but our presentable *parts* have no need. But God composed the body, having given greater honor to that *part* which lacks it, that there should be no schism in the body, but *that* the members should have the same care for one another." (1 Corinthians 12:22-25)

One of the outstanding memories of my youth is a brother in our local church body, who is now with the Lord. Whenever there was a job to do that involved some kind of status, I would feel his hand on my back, nudging me forward. But whenever it was only a matter of hard work, such as mopping the floor, I would normally first become aware that it needed to be done by seeing that he was already doing it. And although under his encouragement I grew to be the teacher and leader he never was, this man was essential to the body, and at the judgment seat of Christ he may indeed receive a greater reward than mine. For I know far more about my own failures than I do about his.

But the Holy Spirit's exhortation here is not only to not think we are more important than others. For He goes on to say:

> "Having then gifts differing according to the grace that is given to us, *let us use them:* if prophecy, *let us prophesy* in proportion to our faith; or ministry, *let us use it* in *our* ministering;

> he who teaches, in teaching; he who exhorts, in exhortation; he who gives, with liberality; he who leads, with diligence; he who shows mercy, with cheerfulness." (Romans 12:6-8)

Some imagine that some kind of human recognition is required for a person to preach the gospel. But that is not what we find here. For the Holy Spirit expressly instructs those that have a spiritual gift to use it. That is, each of us has a personal responsibility to use whatever gift God has given us. As the Apostle Paul said in another place, **"For if I preach the gospel, I have nothing to boast of, for necessity is laid upon me; yes, woe is me if I do not preach the gospel!"** (1 Corinthians 9:16) So we need to realize that this scripture teaches that having a spiritual gift carries with it a responsibility to use that gift.

That responsibility *is* the authority to use that gift. For no action of mankind can either add to or take away from any instruction God has given us. But of course, our God has warned us, **"Beloved, do not believe every spirit, but test the spirits, whether they are of God; because many false prophets have gone out into the world."** (1 John 4:1) And He charges us to judge whatever is proclaimed in the church, rather than simply assuming it is true. **"Let two or three prophets speak, and let the others judge."** (1 Corinthians 14:29) This is a responsibility that rests upon us as individuals. For sadly, many leaders of various church groups endorse not only false teaching, but false teachers. And such false teachers have wormed themselves into positions of leadership in many church groups. This scripture instructs us, as individuals, to judge whatever is being said in the church. We are not to simply assume it is true, but to judge it. And how do we so judge? There is only one standard.

> "To the law and to the testimony! If they do not speak according to this word, *it is* because *there is* no light in them." (Isaiah 8:20)

and

> "All Scripture *is* given by inspiration of God, and *is* profitable for doctrine, for reproof, for correction, for instruction in righteousness, that the man of God may be complete, thoroughly equipped for every good work." (2 Timothy 3:16-17)

The instruction continues in regard to relationships in the church:

> "*Let* love *be* without hypocrisy. Abhor what is evil. Cling to what is good. *Be* kindly affectionate to one another with brotherly love, in honor giving preference to one another; not lagging in diligence, fervent in spirit, serving the Lord; rejoicing in hope, patient in tribulation, continuing steadfastly in prayer; distributing to the needs of the saints, given to hospitality. Bless those who persecute you; bless and do not curse. Rejoice with those who rejoice, and weep with those who weep. Be of the same mind toward one another. Do not set your mind on high things, but associate with the humble. Do not be wise in your own opinion." (Romans 12:9-16)

All these instructions are so direct and simple they need no explanation. They need to be obeyed, not explained.

But then the instruction branches out to relationships outside of the church.

"**Repay no one evil for evil. Have regard for good things in the sight of all men. If it is possible, as much as depends on you, live peaceably with all men. Beloved, do not avenge yourselves, but *rather* give place to wrath; for it is written, 'Vengeance is Mine, I will repay,' says the Lord. Therefore**

'If your enemy is hungry, feed him;

If he is thirsty, give him a drink;

For in so doing you will heap coals of fire on his head.'

Do not be overcome by evil, but overcome evil with good."

(Romans 12:17-21)

Again, these instructions do not need to be explained. They need to be obeyed.

In the next chapter (Romans 13) the instruction widens to our relationship with the government. And sadly, even real Christians often flatly disobey these instructions.

> "Let every soul be subject to the governing authorities. For there is no authority except from God, and the authorities that exist are appointed by God. Therefore whoever resists the authority resists the ordinance of God, and those who resist will bring judgment on themselves. For rulers are not a terror to good works, but to evil. Do you want to be unafraid of the authority? Do what is good, and you will have praise from the same. For he is God's minister to you for good. But if you do evil, be afraid; for he does not bear the sword in vain; for he is God's minister, an avenger to *execute* wrath on him who practices evil. Therefore *you* must be subject, not only because of wrath but also for conscience' sake. For because of this you also pay taxes, for they are God's ministers attending continually to this very thing." (Romans 13:1-6)

Sadly, there are many real Christians who imagine that they owe no obedience to an evil government, totally forgetful of what kind of government was in power when the Holy Spirit gave these instructions. For the government of Rome was openly wicked, endorsing sexual wickedness, practicing slavery, and even going so far as to employ mass murder as entertainment for the masses. And Christians were particular targets of oppression. Yet the Holy Spirit said of *that* government, that **"the authorities that exist are appointed by God."** And commanded believers to **"be subject to the governing authorities."**

Some Christians of our day claim the wickedness of the government as an excuse to refuse to pay taxes. But God himself said concerning the grossly evil government that was in power at that time, **"because of this you also pay taxes, for they are God's ministers."**

So, as Christians, we have zero excuse to fail to pay our taxes or to break the law in any other way, with the sole exception of any time the government orders us to disobey God. In that sole case, we do not gain the right to disobey, but rather, we are required to obey the higher authority. For the authority of God trumps all human authority, regardless of what form that human authority may take. This, by the way, applies not only to relationships between a Christian and the government. It also applies, and perhaps even more strongly, to relationships between an individual Christian and the leadership of whatever church group that individual is connected with. That is, our responsibility to obey God above *all* other authority applies in *all* situations, whether the authority in question is governmental or religious, or for that matter, our employer.

So we are told,

> **"Render therefore to all their due: taxes to whom taxes** *are due***, customs to whom customs, fear to whom fear, honor to whom honor."** (Romans 13:7)

But this is immediately followed by the closely related instruction to

> **"Owe no one anything except to love one another, for he who loves another has fulfilled the law."** (Romans 13:8)

Some have wrested this to be a command to never borrow money, but its connection to what had just been said is obvious. The instruction is to *not fail* to pay whatever is owed. But this is immediately extended to a debt we can never fully pay. For love is a debt that remains, even after it is paid. That is, we always owe love to those around us. And there is never an end to the time when we owe that love.

And then the Holy Spirit explains, saying,

> **"For the commandments, *'You shall not commit adultery,' 'You shall not murder,' 'You shall not steal,' 'You shall not bear false witness,' 'You shall not covet,'* and if *there is* any other commandment, are *all* summed up in this saying, namely, *'You shall love your neighbor as yourself.'* Love does no harm to a neighbor; therefore love is the fulfillment of the law."** (Romans 13:9-10)

So we see that love is really what the law is all about.

These general instructions are completed with the words,

> "And *do* this, knowing the time, that now *it is* high time to awake out of sleep; for now our salvation *is* nearer than when we *first* believed. The night is far spent, the day is at hand. Therefore let us cast off the works of darkness, and let us put on the armor of light. Let us walk properly, as in the day, not in revelry and drunkenness, not in lewdness and lust, not in strife and envy. But put on the Lord Jesus Christ, and make no provision for the flesh, to *fulfill its* lusts." (Romans 13:11-14)

Like so many others of our God's instructions, these do not need to be explained. They need to be obeyed.

The rest of the epistle, up to the conclusion, is specific instruction concerning reception of people into the church group. Some churches will just receive anyone, ignoring clearly stated instructions such as

> "I wrote to you in my epistle not to keep company with sexually immoral people. Yet I certainly did not mean with the sexually immoral people of this world, or with the covetous, or extortioners, or idolaters, since then you would need to go out of the world. But now I have written to you not to keep company with anyone named a brother, who is sexually immoral, or covetous, or an idolater, or a reviler, or a drunkard, or an extortioner--not even to eat with such a person. For what have I to do with judging those also who are outside? Do you not judge those who are inside? But those who are outside God judges. Therefore *'put away from yourselves the evil person.'* " (1 Corinthians 5:9-13)

Other churches will not accept anyone who will not subscribe to some kind of an official statement of doctrine. The application of either of these aberrant concepts is disobedience to the explicit instructions of scripture.

For we are explicitly instructed to

> "**Receive one who is weak in the faith,** *but* **not to disputes over doubtful things.**" (Romans 14:1)

The first part of this instruction is plain enough. But many have a problem with the last part. What is the meaning of **"*but* not to disputes over doubtful things"**? The Greek here is, in our letters, "me eis diakriseis dialogismon," which translates literally, word-for word, as "no into discrimination of-reasonings." The various translations render this various ways. Perhaps the sense is best captured by the English Standard Version, which renders this difficult passage as "but not to quarrel over opinions."

But occupying ourselves overlong on these rather difficult words is really unnecessary. For the Holy Spirit explained His meaning at some length. He did this by two examples, vegetarianism and the observation of specific days, or "holy days," as some call them. And in both of these cases, our God basically told *both* sides to "cool it." We are simply not to argue over such matters.

So we read,

> "**One person believes he may eat anything, while the weak person eats only vegetables. Let not the one who eats despise the one who abstains, and let not the one who abstains pass judgment on the one who eats, for God has welcomed him. Who are you to pass judgment on the servant of another? It is before his own master that he stands or falls. And he will be upheld, for the Lord is able to make him stand. One person esteems one day as better than another, while another esteems all days alike. Each one should be fully convinced in his own mind. The one who observes the day, observes it in honor of the Lord. The one who eats, eats in honor of the Lord, since he gives thanks to God, while the one who abstains, abstains in honor of the Lord and gives thanks to God.**" (Romans 14:2-6)

But we need to remember that this is said in regard to matters of opinion, not in regard to things that are explicitly forbidden by God. Other scriptures plainly instruct us to not tolerate wickedness in our midst. For, as we just noticed, 1 Corinthians 5:11 explicitly forbids us **"even to eat with" "anyone named a brother, who is sexually immoral, or covetous, or an idolater, or a reviler, or a drunkard, or an extortioner."** And 2 John 1:9-10 says that **"If anyone comes to you"** denying **"the doctrine of Christ," "do not receive him into your house nor greet him."** But matters of opinion are something different. And in such matters, we are forbidden to judge the opinions of others.

> **"For none of us lives to himself, and none of us dies to himself. For if we live, we live to the Lord, and if we die, we die to the Lord. So then, whether we live or whether we die, we are the Lord's. For to this end Christ died and lived again, that he might be Lord both of the dead and of the living. Why do you pass judgment on your brother? Or you, why do you despise your brother? For we will all stand before the judgment seat of God; for it is written, 'As I live, says the Lord, every knee shall bow to me, and every tongue shall confess to God.' So then each of us will give an account of himself to God."** (Romans 14:7-12)

So our God's instruction is to wait for the time when God will judge, not only your brother, but also yourself. For each of us will have to give account to God. As the apostle Paul, whom the Holy Spirit used to pen these words, said in another place,

> **"I know nothing against myself, yet I am not justified by this; but He who judges me is the Lord."** (1 Corinthians 4:4)

The Holy Spirit now turns to specific instruction about this concept.

> **"Therefore let us not judge one another anymore, but rather resolve this, not to put a stumbling block or a cause to fall in *our* brother's way. I know and am convinced by the Lord Jesus that *there is* nothing unclean of itself; but to him who considers anything to be unclean, to him *it is* unclean. Yet if your brother is grieved because of *your* food, you are no longer walking in love. Do not destroy with your food the one for whom Christ died. Therefore do not let your good be spoken**

> of as evil; for the kingdom of God is not eating and drinking, but righteousness and peace and joy in the Holy Spirit. Therefore let us pursue the things *which make* for peace and the things by which one may edify another. Do not destroy the work of God for the sake of food. All things indeed *are* pure, but *it is* evil for the man who eats with offense. *It is* good neither to eat meat nor drink wine nor *do anything* by which your brother stumbles or is offended or is made weak. Do you have faith? Have *it* to yourself before God. Happy *is* he who does not condemn himself in what he approves. But he who doubts is condemned if he eats, because *he does* not *eat* from faith; for whatever *is* not from faith is sin." (Romans 14:13-23)

So, instead of judging our brethren for their opinions which we think are mistaken, we should instead be taking care to not cause them to sin. For, even if they are mistaken about what constitutes sinful behavior, if *they* think something is sinful, then, *for them*, it is sinful to do it. So, when we encourage them to do what *they* consider to be sinful, we encourage *them* to sin. And that is why it says, **"Do not destroy with your food the one for who Christ died."** and again, **"Do not destroy the work of God for the sake of food."** And the reason for this is **"the kingdom of God is not eating and drinking, but righteousness and peace and joy in the Holy Spirit."** So, for those who are strong, the specific instruction is, **"*It is* good neither to eat meat nor drink wine nor *do anything* by which your brother stumbles or is offended or is made weak."** And why? Because (for that is what **"for"** means) **"whatsoever is not of faith is sin."** So if you were to encourage a brother to do anything contrary to his own faith before God, you would be encouraging him to sin, and thus destroying both your brother and the work of God in his life.

So in such cases, the specific instruction to those who consider themselves to be strong, is to yield to those whom they consider to be weak. Just give in to their silly opinions, because they are inconsequential anyway. And peace is more important than being right.

"We then who are strong ought to bear with the scruples of the weak, and not to please ourselves. Let each of us please *his* neighbor for *his* good, leading to edification. For even Christ did not please Himself; but as it is written, '*The reproaches of those who reproached You fell on Me.*' For whatever things were written before were written

for our learning, that we through the patience and comfort of the Scriptures might have hope. Now may the God of patience and comfort grant you to be like-minded toward one another, according to Christ Jesus, that you may with one mind *and* one mouth glorify the God and Father of our Lord Jesus Christ. Therefore receive one another, just as Christ also received us, to the glory of God." (Romans 15:1-7)

So all this section, clear back to Romans 14:1, where were told to **"Receive one who is weak in the faith,"** is summarized in one simple statement. **"Therefore receive one another, just as Christ also received us, to the glory of God."** Sadly, some pervert this scripture, pretending it means we should only receive someone *if* that reception would glorify God. But that is exactly the opposite of what this entire section is insisting upon. Instead, the context makes it clear that the meaning of this phrase is that we are to receive each other *because* such reception glorifies God. So those who use this as a pretension to justify excluding other Christians, are flatly disobeying explicitly stated scripture.

And finally, the doctrinal portion of the epistle ends with a proof that the extension of our Lord's blessing to the gentiles was not some kind of a new concept, but had been promised long before to the fathers of Israel. This is proved with four quotations from the Old Testament.

"Now I say that Jesus Christ has become a servant to the circumcision for the truth of God, to confirm the promises *made* to the fathers, and that the Gentiles might glorify God for *His* mercy, as it is written:

'For this reason I will confess to You
among the Gentiles,
And sing to Your name.'
And again he says:
'Rejoice, O Gentiles, with His people!'
And again:
'Praise the LORD, all you Gentiles!'
'Laud Him, all you peoples!'

And again, Isaiah says:
'There shall be a root of Jesse;
And He who shall rise to reign over the Gentiles,
***In Him the Gentiles shall hope.'* "** (Romans 15:8-12)

The first of these quotations is actually stated twice in the Old Testament, first in 2 Samuel 22:50 and then again in Psalms 18:49. The second is quoted from Deuteronomy 32:43. The third is quoted from Psalms 117:1. And the fourth quotation is from Isaiah 11:10.

And finally, the doctrinal portion closes with the words,

> **"Now may the God of hope fill you with all joy and peace in believing, that you may abound in hope by the power of the Holy Spirit."** (Romans 15:13)

CONCLUSION

Chapters 15:14 - 16:27

This rather long conclusion begins with the Apostle explaining why he has written this epistle.

"Now I myself am confident concerning you, my brethren, that you also are full of goodness, filled with all knowledge, able also to admonish one another. Nevertheless, brethren, I have written more boldly to you on *some* points, as reminding you, because of the grace given to me by God, that I might be a minister of Jesus Christ to the Gentiles, ministering the gospel of God, that the offering of the Gentiles might be acceptable, sanctified by the Holy Spirit. Therefore I have reason to glory in Christ Jesus in the things *which pertain* to God. For I will not dare to speak of any of those things which Christ has not accomplished through me, in word and deed, to make the Gentiles obedient-- in mighty signs and wonders, by the power of the Spirit of God, so that from Jerusalem and round about to Illyricum I have fully preached the gospel of Christ. And so I have made it my aim to preach the gospel, not where Christ was named, lest I should build on another man's foundation, but as it is written: *'To whom He was not announced, they shall see; And those who have not heard shall understand.'* " (Romans 15:14-21)

The Holy Spirit first led the Apostle to reassure the Romans that this epistle had not been because they were spiritually ignorant, but only because they needed to be reminded of these things. As was noted in the beginning of this book, this kind of sensitivity to people's feelings was often used by the Holy Spirit in giving us the scriptures. To those who were in rebellion, His words were almost always harsh and condemning. But to those desirous of faithfully following Him, the Holy Spirit's words are gentle, even when He needs to correct them. So the instructive portions of this epistle are sandwiched between statements of encouragement and praise for the people being instructed.

Then we are told the basic mission of Paul, as an Apostle of Jesus Christ. His commission was to preach the gospel where it had never before been preached. And again, an Old Testament scripture is quoted to show that this had been part of God's plan all along, from the very beginning. The quotation is from Isaiah 52:15, where God had concluded a short (three verse) prophecy about our Lord's prudence and suffering by saying

"what had not been told them they shall see,

And what they had not heard they shall consider."

Next, the Apostle's current plans are discussed in verses 22-32. We need to note that the last part of these plans may indeed have been the desire of the Holy Spirit. But completion of these plans was rendered impossible by Paul's refusal to obey the Spirit's directive to cancel his intended trip to Jerusalem. We should here note that, although it might seem to have still been the Spirit's intention for Paul to go to Jerusalem, even though he had been repeatedly warned of what awaited him there, we are finally told in Acts 21:5 that the disciples in Tyre **"told Paul through the Spirit not to go up to Jerusalem."** So we are indeed not only told that the Holy Spirit repeatedly warned Paul of what would happen there, but that He finally explicitly told him **"not to go up to Jerusalem."** And it was Paul's disobedience to this clearly stated instruction that prevented the rest of these plans from being completed, and negated the prayers he had requested **"that I may be delivered from those in Judea who do not believe."** (Romans 15:31) For our God usually refuses to deliver us from the natural results of our disobedience.

This, like the failures of Peter we are told about, serves to warn us that even the best of us often fail. And when we begin to have confidence in ourselves, our Lord often allows a test that He knows we will fail. It is in this way that He trains us to be totally dependant upon Himself. And this may indeed be the reason the Holy Spirit led Paul to reveal these plans, which never came to pass, even though Paul was certain they would, as he said in verse 29,

> **"But I know that when I come to you, I shall come in the fullness of the blessing of the gospel of Christ."**

Chapter 16, the last chapter of this epistle, begins with a commendation of a beloved sister named Phoebe. And then the next fifteen verses are greetings to various individuals in Rome. This is followed a few verses later by greetings being sent from various individuals that were with Paul. Some may imagine that such material is useless today. But if nothing else, it shows our God's interest in us as individuals. Not only are these two groups of Christians noticed as groups, but many of the various individuals among them are also singled out for particular mention.

But between these two sections we find a final warning:

> **"Now I urge you, brethren, note those who cause divisions and offenses, contrary to the doctrine which you learned, and avoid them. For those who are such do not serve our Lord Jesus Christ, but their own belly, and by smooth words and flattering speech deceive the hearts of the simple. For your obedience has become known to all. Therefore I am glad on your behalf; but I want you to be wise in what is good, and simple concerning evil. And the God of peace will crush Satan under your feet shortly. The grace of our Lord Jesus Christ** *be* **with you. Amen."** (Romans 16:17-20)

The discipline which the church is here exhorted to apply is not the exclusion commanded for those professing the name of Christ, but living wicked lives, as is explicitly commanded in 1 Corinthians 5:1-14, or for those denying fundamental doctrine, as is explicitly commanded in 2 John 1:9-11. Here, divisive persons are simply to be avoided. That is, we are not to seek out their company, nor to accept their attempts befriend us. And why? **"For those who are such do not serve our Lord Jesus Christ, but their own belly."** And the Holy Spirit wants His saints **"to be wise in what is good, and simple concerning evil."** And they are left with a final word of comfort, that **"the God of peace will crush Satan under your feet shortly."**

And they are told, twice over, **"The grace of our Lord Jesus Christ *be* with you."** before the epistle ends in a magnificent doxology:

> **"Now to Him who is able to establish you according to my gospel and the preaching of Jesus Christ, according to the revelation of the mystery kept secret since the world began but now has been made manifest, and by the prophetic Scriptures has been made known to all nations, according to the commandment of the everlasting God, for obedience to the faith-- to God, alone wise, *be* glory through Jesus Christ forever. Amen."** (Romans 16:25-27)

This, although it is indeed a doxology, that is, a grand statement of praise to God, is more than a simple doxology. For it also refers to important doctrine. For there had been a **"mystery kept secret since the world began."** But this **"mystery"** had now **"been made manifest, and by the prophetic Scriptures has been made known to all nations."**

We are not told in this place what this **"mystery"** was. But we are told in Ephesians 3:6 that it was

> **"that the Gentiles should be fellow heirs, of the same body, and partakers of His promise in Christ through the gospel."**

And in that place we are explicitly told, as we are here in the conclusion of the Epistle to the Romans, that this **"mystery"**

"in other ages was not made known to the sons of men, as it has now been revealed by the Spirit to His holy apostles and prophets:" (Ephesians 3:5)

Why is this important? Because it shows that **"the church"** being a single body composed of both Jews and Gentiles was never revealed in the Old Testament. And thus we understand that the many Old Testament scriptures making promises to **"Israel"** actually meant **"Israel,"** and not **"the church."** Because **"the church"** is a body never revealed in *any* Old Testament scripture. And thus, at the very end of this rather long conclusion, is summed up the doctrine developed in such detail in chapters 9 to 11 of this most important book of the Bible.

Trust Publishers House,
the trusted name in quality Christian books.

Trust House Publishers
PO Box 3181
Taos, NM 87571

TrustHousePublishers.com

www.ingramcontent.com/pod-product-compliance
Lightning Source LLC
Chambersburg PA
CBHW052111110526
44592CB00013B/1562